The
Ultimate
Best Friend's
Guide

The
Ultimate
Best Friend's
Guide:

Mastering the Art of Friendship

Amber Ahava
With
Trees United

Also available for purchase is the companion journal to complement this book.
Enjoy!

Table of Contents
Ideas on " How to Be the Best Friend "

Forward

Forward

Friendship is one of the most profound gifts we can give and receive in life. Relationships transcend the boundaries of time, place, and circumstance, grounding us in a shared understanding of joy, struggle, and everything in between. It is often said that friends are the family we choose for ourselves, and this simple truth reveals the incredible strength and depth that friendships can offer.

This book is an exploration of that bond. It delves into the ways friendship shapes us, challenges us, and helps us grow. Through stories of laughter, loyalty, heartbreak, and healing, the pages ahead will remind you of the beauty in these connections. Whether you're reminiscing about old friends, forging new ones, or reflecting on the ways in which friendships have altered the course of your life, this collection invites you to celebrate the friendships that have touched your heart.

Friendship is one of the deepest, most transformative relationships we experience as human beings. It is often said that the friends we have are the mirror in which we see ourselves; reflecting not just who we are, but who we strive to be. It is through the lens of friendship that we learn how to navigate life's complexities—our joy, our pain, our failures, and our triumphs. But more than that, friendship teaches us about the art of being human, the delicate balance between giving and receiving, between supporting and allowing ourselves to be supported. It is, in its most authentic form, a journey of mutual care and respect.

Yet, being a truly great friend—someone who can offer support, love, and comfort in times of need, and someone who can challenge, grow, and inspire—requires more than just the desire to be kind. It requires intention, effort, and a willingness to reflect upon and nurture the many qualities that make a friendship thrive. This guidebook is dedicated to helping you become the ultimate best friend: one who excels at empathy, listening, consistency, honesty, kindness, respect, boundaries, grace, apologizing, and encouragement. These are the cornerstones that not only fortify the foundation of friendship but make it one that is lasting, meaningful, and resilient.

Friendship is not just an emotion; it is a foundation upon which our lives are built. It is one of the few human experiences that transcends time, space, and circumstance, anchoring us in ways that are often immeasurable. It exists in the shared laughter between old friends, in the quiet understanding between those who know us best, and in the moments of vulnerability when we seek solace and strength in the presence of another.

But what is the true meaning of friendship? Is it merely the mutual enjoyment of each other's company, or is there something deeper—a bond that transcends the good times and endures through hardship and change? To understand the essence of friendship, we must not only examine the joys and pleasures it brings but also reflect on its challenges and complexities. True friendship, as we have explored throughout this book, is not simply a passive exchange of affection—it is an active, evolving force that requires empathy, trust, honesty, boundaries, and resilience. It is a dynamic relationship, one that asks us to grow as individuals, challenge our assumptions, and extend grace to one another.

As we reflect on the friendships that have shaped our lives, we come to realize that the essence of friendship is found not in grand gestures, but in the quiet, consistent acts of love and care. It is found in the willingness to listen, to be present in times of joy and sorrow, and to support one another through life's many twists and turns. But more than anything, the truest form of friendship is found in the understanding that, despite our flaws, we are worthy of love, and that through our relationships with others, we learn to love ourselves.

The people we call friends help us discover parts of ourselves we might never know otherwise. They are there for us when we need a shoulder to cry on, an ear to listen, or simply a companion to share in the joys of life. In their presence, we are reminded that we are not alone in this world. This book is dedicated to those who have walked alongside us, making the journey worthwhile.

As you turn these pages, may you be inspired to reach out, reconnect, and deepen the friendships and all relationships that make your world brighter. For in the end, it's these relationships that enrich our lives more than anything else.

Introduction

Friendships Matter

Friendship is one of the few constants in life that enriches us beyond measure. The people we call friends have a unique place in our lives; they are the ones we confide in, laugh with, lean on, and celebrate our triumphs with. True and meaningful friendships add an irreplaceable depth to our lives, influencing our well-being, self-identity, and sense of purpose. Yet, as common as the concept of friendship is, deep and meaningful friendships are rare, and they require intentional effort and appreciation.

In today's fast-paced world, where connections are often measured by social media metrics rather than genuine understanding, nurturing authentic friendships can seem challenging. But it is precisely in this environment that the value of real friends, those with whom we can be our true selves, stands out. The journey to being a true friend starts with understanding what friendship truly means and acknowledging its powerful impact on our lives.

Mindful Well-being

Research across the fields of psychology and sociology has consistently shown the positive effects of friendship on mental health. While family relationships certainly play a vital role, friends often occupy a special place in our lives. Friendships are usually relationships of choice rather than obligation, this creates a uniquely supportive and affirming space.

True friendships act as a buffer against life's inevitable hardships. When we're faced with stressors like job changes, health issues, or personal disappointments, having a friend who listens without judgment and offers perspective can lessen the impact of those experiences. In times of sadness or struggle, the simple act of spending time with a friend, even in silence, can be profoundly comforting. Reminding us that we are not alone in our experiences and that our feelings are understood. This sense of being "seen" without needing to justify our emotions is a critical factor in mental resilience.

Studies show that having meaningful friendships can reduce anxiety and depression. Talking with friends allows us to process complex emotions, make sense of our challenges, and often see situations from a different angle. This support doesn't always need to come in the form of advice; sometimes, it's about the unspoken understanding that someone is there, willing to listen and share in the journey.

Can Friendships Shape Our Sense of Identity

Beyond their effect on our mental health, friendships play a crucial role in shaping who we are. Our friends influence our choices, interests, and even our values in subtle but significant ways. While this can happen unconsciously, the friends we choose often reflect parts of ourselves; our values, our priorities, and the people we aspire to be.

Consider how our friendships evolve over time. In childhood, friends often come from shared proximity or activities, but as we grow, our friendships tend to deepen around shared values and life experiences. Friends become mirrors that reflect aspects of ourselves and they often encourage us to grow in directions we might not have considered on our own. Through the validation and encouragement of friends, we develop self-confidence, are more willing to take risks, and feel supported in exploring new interests and goals.

Our friends offer perspectives that broaden our understanding of the world. Through their eyes, we can see beyond our immediate experiences, which enriches our worldview and challenges us to think in new ways. Good friends often serve as a reality check, helping us stay grounded. When we find ourselves drifting or losing perspective, a friend's honest insight can act as an anchor, reminding us of who we are and the values we hold dear.

A Source of Joy and Purpose

One of the most beautiful aspects of friendship is the joy it brings. Shared laughter, spontaneous adventures, or even a quiet afternoon spent together can bring a level of happiness that is hard to find elsewhere. True friends make the highs in life higher and the lows more bearable. In a world that sometimes feels focused on productivity and achievement, friendships provide a rare space where simply "being" is enough.

This joy contributes to a sense of purpose. Knowing that someone relies on you or appreciates your presence can be profoundly fulfilling. Friendships offer opportunities to be needed, to give without expectation, and to contribute positively to another person's life. In many ways, being a good friend allows us to focus on the well-being of others, which helps cultivate qualities like kindness, empathy, and generosity. These qualities, in turn, enhance our self-worth and make us feel more connected to the world around us.

Resilience and Adaptability

Life, as we all know, is unpredictable. The world is filled with changes that we cannot always prepare for, and in these times, friends become anchors and motivators. While family may provide a safety net, friends offer a kind of support that is free from familial obligations, allowing us to be more open and vulnerable. Friends who have seen us at our best and worst are invaluable because they remind us of our strength during difficult times. They have witnessed our struggles and growth, and their support can reignite our hope when we lose faith in ourselves.

True friendships foster resilience by giving us a safe space to process our experiences and then move forward. This adaptability is essential, especially as we face life's many transitions. Transitions from career changes to relationships, health issues, or aging. Friends often become an unofficial advisory board in times of uncertainty, providing perspectives that we may not be able to see on our own. Just knowing that someone has our back, believes in us, and can see us through our challenges bolsters our ability to adapt and move forward with confidence.

Physical Health Benefits of Friendships

The benefits of friendships extend beyond mental and emotional health; they also have measurable effects on physical health. Studies have shown that individuals with strong social ties live longer, have stronger immune systems, and are less prone to chronic conditions like heart disease. Close friendships can actually decrease our levels of cortisol, the stress hormone that is often linked to various health issues when elevated over long periods.

Spending time with friends can also encourage healthier habits. Friends can motivate us to stick to positive routines, whether it's exercising together, cooking healthy meals, or reminding each other of self-care routines. A friend's influence is often more motivating than personal discipline alone.
The social engagement that comes from being with friends, even for a simple activity like a walk, has been shown to improve cardiovascular health and reduce risk factors for many diseases.

A Reflection of Our Humanity

Friendships touch something fundamentally human within us. Unlike most other relationships, which can sometimes be defined by duty or social structure, friendship is purely a choice. We choose friends not out of obligation but because we feel a connection, an affinity, and a desire to share our lives with them. This choice makes friendship one of the most authentic bonds in our lives.

The act of being a friend teaches us humility, patience, forgiveness, and gratitude. Through the ups and downs of friendships, we come to understand our own capacity for compassion. Friends show us that we are capable of being there for someone else in a way that's meaningful and impactful. In turn, this deepens our sense of self, as we learn what we value in others and what we are willing to give of ourselves.

Relationships reflect our humanity by allowing us to experience the world through someone else's eyes. Each friend offers us a unique perspective, enriching our lives in ways we often don't realize until we take a moment to reflect on it. This shared experience of being human, with all its joy, challenges, and uncertainties, binds us in a way that transcends other relationships.

The Legacy

When we look back on our lives, friendships often form the backbone of our fondest memories. These are the people who have walked with us through every season, contributing to our sense of fulfillment and meaning. The laughter, the shared experiences, the mutual support, these are the things that linger long after the moments have passed.

Relationships are our legacy. They impact not only our lives but also the lives of those around us, as we often find that our friendships influence how we treat others, our outlook on life, and even the values we pass on. By cultivating true, meaningful friendships, we contribute to a legacy of kindness and understanding that has the power to ripple through generations.

The journey to becoming the best friend is not about grand gestures or perfection. It is about consistently showing up, listening, caring, and being present. When we strive to be the best friend we can be, we contribute not only to our own well-being but to a broader culture of empathy and connection that benefits everyone.

The value of deep, meaningful friendships cannot be overstated. They nurture our mental and physical health, shape our identities, and add richness to our lives in ways few other relationships can. As we embark on

the journey to understand what it means to be the best friend, we realize
that friendship is as much a gift to others as it is to ourselves.
True friendship is a testament to the beauty of human connection, a bond
that holds the potential to transform lives in profound ways.

Chapter 1

Empathy and Active Listening

In the world of friendships, empathy and active listening are the foundations upon which trust, intimacy, and genuine connection are built. While many qualities make someone a great friend, few are as essential or transformative as the ability to empathize and to listen. In this chapter, we'll dive deep into the role that empathy and active listening play in strengthening friendships, explore what these concepts truly mean, and discuss practical ways to practice them with those we care about.

Empathy goes beyond merely understanding another person's experience; it is the capacity to feel alongside them, to see the world from their perspective, and to create a bridge between two different experiences. Active listening, on the other hand, is the skill of fully immersing oneself in a conversation, showing attentiveness, and responding in a way that demonstrates understanding and care. When combined, empathy and active listening create an environment where friends feel seen, heard, and valued. In a world that often feels noisy and disconnected, these qualities are more essential than ever.

Empathy is one of the most misunderstood yet powerful components of a deep friendship. In simple terms, empathy is the ability to put yourself in another person's shoes, feeling as they feel and understanding what they are going through. Real empathy in friendship goes further than this. True empathy requires us to step outside our own experiences, suspending our judgments and preconceived notions. It asks us to understand the emotions of our friends' individuality without our own biases clouding the view.

There are three main types of empathy: cognitive empathy, emotional empathy, and compassionate empathy. Cognitive empathy is the intellectual understanding of another's perspective. A knowing of what they feel without necessarily sharing the emotion. Emotional empathy is when we share the emotional experience of another person, feeling their happiness or sadness within ourselves. Lastly, compassionate empathy involves understanding and sharing in the emotional experience while also being moved to help or support in any way we can. In friendships, we often shift between these types of empathy. But it is typically compassionate empathy that fosters the deepest bonds.

When we approach friendships with empathy, we create a safe space for our friends to express themselves without fear of being judged or misunderstood. Empathy tells our friends, "I am here with you, not to fix or judge, but to understand and support." This approach builds a level of trust and openness that is hard to achieve in any other way. In fact, research shows that people who feel empathized with are more likely to open up and share their inner world, leading to stronger, more fulfilling friendships.

Empathy has an Impact

Empathy matters and has real-life impacts on our friendships. In friendship it is about more than just listening; it's about validating a friend's experience, making them feel understood, and building a foundation of trust that can withstand the inevitable challenges of life. When a friend knows that you "get" them, that you understand their feelings and reactions without judgment, they are more likely to turn to you during difficult times. This level of understanding creates a deeper bond, one that goes beyond surface-level interactions and into a territory where both friends feel free to be vulnerable.

For example, consider a friend going through a difficult breakup. It can be tempting to give advice or offer clichés like "There are plenty of fish in the sea" or "Time heals all wounds." While well-meaning, such responses can sometimes feel dismissive. And they may inadvertently make your friend

feel misunderstood. Empathy, however, calls for a different approach. Instead of trying to fix the problem or gloss over the pain, empathy encourages us to sit with our friend in their sadness.
It also acknowledges the depth of their feelings and gives them the space to express those feelings openly.

When we offer empathy in moments like these, we communicate that our friend's pain matters to us. This simple but profound act of acknowledgment allows friends to feel validated, safe, and cared for. These experiences create lasting memories and forge a bond of trust that is hard to break. In the long run, friends who know they can rely on each other for empathetic support are more likely to invest in and prioritize the friendship. This creates a cycle of mutual care and understanding that strengthens the relationship over time.

Sarah and Olivia had been friends for years, but when Sarah's father passed away, she found herself in a deep fog of grief. Olivia, despite never having experienced a similar loss, was determined to support her friend. She didn't have all the answers or know exactly what to say, but what she did have was an open heart and a willingness to be there, no matter what.

She'd show up on Sarah's doorstep with coffee and a comforting presence. Some days, she'd just sit in silence, knowing that sometimes, it's the act of being present that counts the most. Olivia didn't try to fix Sarah's pain; she simply offered her empathy by holding space for Sarah's sorrow. It was in these small, quiet moments that Sarah felt truly understood. Olivia's empathetic support didn't diminish Sarah's grief, but it allowed her to face it without feeling alone.

At the core of any strong friendship is empathy, an ability to understand and share in the feelings of another. Empathy is not just about being able to offer a shoulder to cry on; it's about truly walking in the other person's shoes. It means suspending judgment and being present in their emotional experience. When you show up for your friend with empathy, you give them the gift of being truly seen, truly heard, and truly understood. It's a powerful way of connecting with another human being, and one that often requires deep vulnerability.

Empathy isn't just about comforting your friend when things go wrong. It also means celebrating their victories with them. When you can feel joy in their successes, without jealousy or competition, it is a testament to the selfless nature of friendship. True empathy encourages growth, mutual support, and shared happiness.

Power of Active Listening

Active listening is an art. One of the most powerful yet overlooked skills in any friendship. While listening might seem straightforward, truly active listening requires intentionality, presence, and a willingness to put aside our own thoughts and reactions. Active listening is about more than just hearing words. It's about understanding the emotions, needs, and unspoken meanings behind those words.

To be an active listener means to be fully present in the conversation. This involves making eye contact, nodding, asking follow-up questions, and responding in a way that shows genuine interest and engagement. It also means resisting the urge to interrupt, give advice, or steer the conversation toward our own experiences. Instead, active listening is about creating a space for the speaker to feel fully heard and understood.

One of the key components of active listening is reflection. Reflection involves repeating back what you've heard in your own words to confirm your understanding. Like when a friend shares how stressed they've been at work, you might respond by saying, "It sounds like you've been feeling really overwhelmed with everything that's on your plate."
This simple act of reflection shows that you are not only listening but also genuinely trying to understand your friend's experience. It encourages them to go deeper and share more. It allows them to know that you are truly engaged and interested in what they have to say.

Active listening has many benefits and strengthens friendships in numerous ways. First, it builds trust. When friends know they can come to you and be heard without judgment, it makes them more likely to confide in you and trust you with their deeper thoughts and feelings. This trust becomes the backbone of a lasting friendship. One where both parties feel safe to be their true selves.

This type of active listening fosters mutual respect. When we listen attentively, we show that we value our friend's thoughts, feelings, and experiences. This kind of respect is essential for a balanced friendship; where both parties feel equally valued and appreciated.

Lastly, active listening helps to prevent misunderstandings and conflicts. Many disagreements stem from miscommunication or assumptions. By practicing active listening, we ensure that we fully understand our friend's perspective before responding. This clarity can prevent small issues from escalating into larger conflicts. It makes both people feel heard and understood from the beginning.

Jasmine and Lucy had always been the best of friends, but their paths had diverged in recent years. Jasmine had taken a job in a different city, and though they stayed in touch, it wasn't the same. One evening, Jasmine called Lucy, clearly overwhelmed by the stress of a big presentation at work. Lucy, despite being busy with her own life, immediately put everything aside to listen.

Instead of offering advice or trying to solve Jasmine's problems, Lucy gave her her full attention. She listened intently, asking questions when needed, and allowed Jasmine to vent her frustrations. At the end of the conversation, Jasmine felt better—not because Lucy had told her what to do, but because Lucy had given her the space to voice her thoughts and emotions without judgment.

Helpful Ideas to Cultivate Empathy and Active Listening

Building empathy and active listening skills takes practice, especially if we're not used to focusing our full attention on others. Here are some helpful ideas to help strengthen these qualities in your friendships:

1. **Practice Mindfulness**: Mindfulness is the art of being present in the moment. By practicing mindfulness, we train ourselves to focus on the present conversation, setting aside distractions and our own internal dialogue. This presence is essential for both empathy and active listening.

2. **Ask Open-Ended Questions**: When engaging with a friend, try to ask questions that encourage them to share more about their experience. For example, instead of asking, "Are you okay?" you might ask, "How have you been feeling about everything lately?" Open-ended questions show that you're interested in more than just a surface-level response and invite your friend to express themselves freely.

3. **Resist the Urge to Fix**: Often, our instinct is to solve problems or offer solutions, especially when we see a friend in pain. However, empathy requires us to set aside this impulse and simply be present. Sometimes, the best thing we can do is listen without trying to change or fix anything.

4. **Reflect and Validate**: Reflection is a powerful tool in active listening. By repeating back what you've heard, you demonstrate that you're paying attention and understanding their words. Validation goes hand-in-hand with reflection, as it involves acknowledging their feelings and letting them know their emotions are valid and understandable.

5. **Check Your Biases and Assumptions**: True empathy requires us to set aside our own judgments and assumptions. When listening to a friend, be aware of any biases or preconceived notions that might color your understanding. Approach the conversation with an open mind, allowing your friend to share their experience without feeling judged.

6. **Follow Up**: One of the simplest but most meaningful ways to show empathy is by following up on a conversation later. If a friend shared a concern or mentioned something they were struggling with, reach out a few days later to check in. This follow-up shows that you genuinely care and that their experience matters to you.

When Empathy and Active Listening Are Challenging

While empathy and active listening are essential qualities in any friendship, there will inevitably be times when they feel challenging. Life's stresses, personal differences, or even our own emotional fatigue can make it difficult to fully engage with our friends in the way we'd like. During these times, it's important to remember that empathy and active listening are skills that can be developed with patience and self-compassion.
If you find yourself struggling to empathize with a friend's experience, take a step back and consider what might be causing this difficulty. Are you dealing with your own stress or feeling overwhelmed by other responsibilities? It's okay to acknowledge these feelings and communicate them to your friend. Authenticity is key in any friendship, and sometimes, simply letting your friend know that you're not in the best headspace to listen deeply can prevent misunderstandings and foster transparency.

Empathy and active listening may also be challenging when a friend's experience is vastly different from our own. In these cases, it can be helpful to approach the conversation with curiosity rather than judgment. Instead of focusing on the differences, look for universal emotions or themes that you can relate to. For example, if a friend is going through a challenging experience that you've never encountered, try to relate by considering a time when you felt similar emotions, even if the circumstances were different.

When we approach friendships with empathy and active listening, we create a foundation of trust and understanding that can withstand the ups and downs of life. This has a lasting impact on our relationships. Friends who feel truly heard and valued are more likely to invest in the friendship, creating a positive cycle of mutual care and respect.

Empathy and active listening are not just skills; they are gifts that we give to each other. Gifts that allow us to connect on a deeply human level. In a world that often encourages us to focus on ourselves, these qualities remind us of the beauty of selflessness and the importance of being there for others. As we practice empathy and active listening in our friendships, we not only become better friends but also become better versions of ourselves—more compassionate, patient, and understanding.

Listening is an essential, yet often overlooked, component of being a great friend. Too often in our fast-paced, multitasking world, we find ourselves distracted only half-listening while our minds race ahead. But listening, in its truest form, is an active, engaged process. It requires us to put aside our own thoughts and truly hear what the other person is saying, not just with our ears but with our hearts.

When you listen to a friend, it means giving them your full attention. It means asking thoughtful questions, giving feedback, and offering insight that shows you care. But above all, listening means creating a space where your friend feels safe to express themselves without fear of judgment or interruption. Sometimes, listening is not just about hearing words—it's about tuning into the unsaid emotions and the quiet spaces between the lines.

Ultimately, active listening and empathy are what transform a casual friendship into a true lifelong bond. They allow us to see our friends for who they are. To support them in ways that are meaningful and lasting. Through the practice of empathy and active listening, we create friendships that are not only enriching but also deeply fulfilling. Friendships that bring joy, resilience, and purpose to our lives.

Chapter 2

Reliability and Consistency

Building and sustaining a meaningful friendship isn't solely about shared interests or occasional laughter; it's rooted in qualities that establish a strong, reliable foundation. Among these, the virtues of presence, dependability, and consistency stand out as essential. These qualities form the bedrock of any friendship, creating a space where trust and mutual respect can thrive. A friend who is genuinely present, someone who shows up dependably and remains consistent, offers something invaluable. This type of friendship offers a steady, grounding relationship that endures over time.

Being present means more than just physical proximity; it's about showing up mentally and emotionally, focusing fully on our friend, and being there when they need us. Dependability signals that a friend can rely on us in times of need or celebration. Consistency demonstrates that we are there not only in good times but through life's natural fluctuations. Together, these traits can foster a friendship that is not only fulfilling but resilient, capable of enduring the highs and lows that inevitably come.

Presence in friendship is powerful and about more than simply being around. It's about creating space for another person in our lives, offering our undivided attention and emotional support. In a world filled with distractions, from busy schedules to technology vying for our attention, true presence has become a rare and cherished quality. To be truly present for a friend means setting aside our own thoughts, concerns, and external distractions. Allowing ourselves to be fully engaged in the moment with them. It is an intentional act of prioritizing someone else, of listening, empathizing, and understanding.

Being present conveys to our friends that they matter. When we are fully attentive, we communicate respect and appreciation. A friend who feels that they have our full attention is more likely to open up, trust, and deepen their connection with us. Presence nurtures intimacy, creating a safe environment where friends feel valued and understood. Whether we're sharing in their joy or supporting them through challenges; our presence is a powerful affirmation of their importance in our lives.

Our presence in friendship can be healing. When a friend is going through a difficult time, there is often little we can say to ease their pain. However, simply being there, offering a listening ear or a comforting hug, speaks volumes. This silent support can be more meaningful than any words. Often, it's the quiet presence of a friend that reminds us we are not alone, that someone cares, and that we have the strength to face our challenges.

Dependability in friendship is a cornerstone of trust. It plays a crucial role in strengthening relational bonds. When we say we'll be there and actually follow through, we build credibility and reliability in our relationships. This reassures our friends that they can count on us in both small moments and big life events. A friend we can count on becomes a pillar of stability. Someone we know will answer when we call, show up when they promise, and be there when times get tough.

Being dependable isn't only about showing up for the grand gestures; it's about consistency in the small acts that build up over time. For example, a friend who regularly checks in, remembers important dates, or notices when something seems off is quietly telling us that they are there for us in every sense. This consistent presence lays a foundation of trust that runs deep. When friends know they can rely on each other in small matters, they are more likely to turn to each other in moments of crisis or vulnerability, knowing they'll find support.

To display these characteristics we must keep our word. In any friendship, there will be times when we make promises, whether explicitly or implicitly. When we follow through, we strengthen the trust in the relationship. However, if we fail to keep our promises, even unintentionally, it can slowly erode trust. Dependability, therefore, is built on integrity and follow-through, qualities that every strong friendship requires.

A steady foundation in friendship consistency is often overlooked, but it is the glue that holds all other qualities together. A friend who is consistent is one who offers steady companionship, one who has a remaining presence regardless of life's inevitable changes. This assures us that our friend will be there not only during moments of excitement or ease but also in the everyday or challenging times.

Inconsistency, on the other hand, can introduce uncertainty. A friend who is hot and cold or only shows up sporadically can make us feel like we're walking on eggshells, unsure of where we stand. Reliable stability provides a sense of security in friendship. It tells us that, even as life changes, there are people who will be there for us, steady and unwavering. Steady friends create a sense of continuity, a reminder that no matter what we face, there are constants we can rely on.

Consistency is particularly important in today's fast-paced world, where commitments often feel fluid and priorities frequently shift. Friendships that lack consistency can feel temporary, while those that are built on regular, dependable presence foster a sense of permanence. Persistent friends are the ones who call or check in regularly, who celebrate our victories and share in our sorrows without disappearing when life gets complicated. This stability becomes a source of comfort, reminding us that no matter what changes, our friend remains a steady and grounding presence.

When presence, dependability, and consistency are present in a friendship, they create a strong bond that is rooted in trust and respect. These qualities allow friends to feel secure, knowing they can be themselves without fear of abandonment or judgment. This trust deepens the connection, encouraging each person to invest more fully in the relationship.

For example, consider a friend who is going through a difficult time. A friend who is present will listen attentively, allowing the person to express their emotions freely. Will dependably follow up, offering support not just in the moment but over time. And a friend who is consistent will remain by their side, providing ongoing support even as time passes. Together, these qualities create a friendship that is both nurturing and resilient.

There is a saying that trust is built in drops and broken in buckets. In friendship, consistency is the drop-by-drop foundation of trust. A great friend shows up, time and time again, not just when it's convenient or when life is easy, but especially when it's hard. Whether it's a phone call when you know they need support, a message to check in, or simply a willingness to stand by their side, consistency is what allows friendships to flourish.

Reliability in a friend doesn't mean being perfect; it means being dependable, showing up when you say you will, and being there for the long haul. Life changes, people change, but a great friend remains steadfast. They don't promise perfection, but they promise presence and dedication, and that is the hallmark of true loyalty.

Presence, dependability, and consistency also help friends navigate conflicts and misunderstandings. Every friendship will encounter disagreements, but when both friends trust each other and know they can rely on each other, they are more likely to approach conflicts with patience and understanding. This level of mutual respect allows friends to address issues openly and honestly, rather than letting small grievances build up into resentment.

Amelia was the kind of friend who always came through in a pinch. When Maya's car broke down late one evening in a part of town she wasn't familiar with, she immediately called Amelia. Without hesitation, Amelia grabbed her keys and drove across the city to help. Even though it was late, and she had an early morning meeting, Amelia showed up, offering not just a ride, but a sense of calm.

Maya knew that no matter the time or situation, Amelia would always be there when she needed her. Amelia's reliability and steadfast presence made Maya feel secure and valued in their friendship.

Cultivating Presence, Dependability, and Consistency in Friendships

While these qualities are vital, cultivating them requires conscious effort and intentionality. Here are six practical insights to embody these traits in your friendships:

1. **Prioritize Quality Time**: Being present requires us to set aside dedicated time for our friends. Try to carve out moments where you can focus fully on them, free from distractions like phones or other obligations. This could mean regular catch-ups over coffee, phone calls, or even spontaneous outings.

2. **Follow Through on Commitments**: Dependability is about honoring your word. If you say you'll be there, make it a priority. In cases where you genuinely can't follow through, communicate openly and honestly, showing your friend that you respect their time and trust.

3. **Create Rituals or Routines**: Consistency can be cultivated by establishing regular touchpoints with friends. This could mean scheduling a weekly or monthly call, setting up recurring meet-ups, or simply making it a habit to check in regularly. These routines provide a steady rhythm that reinforces the relationship over time.

4. **Be Mindful of Small Actions**: Sometimes, it's the little things that show we care. Sending a quick text to check in, remembering important events, or following up after a difficult conversation demonstrates that we are attentive and engaged in the friendship.

5. **Communicate Openly**: If there are times when being present, dependable, or consistent is challenging due to personal circumstances, let

your friend know. Authentic communication fosters understanding and helps prevent misunderstandings or hurt feelings.

6. **Stay Engaged During Conversations**: When spending time with a friend, make an effort to be fully engaged. Ask questions, show interest, and listen attentively. This not only strengthens the bond but shows your friend that you genuinely value their presence.

Friendships that are rooted in presence, dependability, and consistency often become life-long connections. These are the friendships that endure beyond seasons of life, that remain constant through change. And that offers comfort and stability in a world that can often feel unpredictable.

As we go through life, we inevitably face challenges, joys, and transitions. Friends who are present, dependable, and consistent become a constant support system. Reminding us of who we are and where we come from. They offer a sense of continuity that is invaluable, providing a steady foundation amidst life's ever-shifting landscape.

These friendships also serve as a powerful reminder of our own capacity for connection and loyalty. By being a friend who embodies these qualities, we contribute to a culture of caring and commitment, inspiring others to do the same. In this way, presence, dependability, and consistency not only strengthen individual friendships but contribute to a broader sense of community and support.

Presence, dependability, and consistency are qualities that require intentional effort but yield invaluable rewards. Friendships with impact that are built on these foundations are resilient, deeply fulfilling, and capable of withstanding life's inevitable ups and downs. These qualities form a legacy of trust and loyalty. Traits we can all long for in this fast paced, instant gratification society we live in. The provision of someone we can count on no matter what is a thing most of us desire at some point in life. Let us start to build these kinds of legacies for our future and present well-being. Building a legacy of trust and loyalty. It begins with you and me.

Chapter 3

Honesty with Kindness

Trust is the invisible thread that binds friendships together, weaving a sense of safety, respect, and loyalty between two people. Without trust, a friendship lacks stability and depth; with it, friendships can withstand misunderstandings, conflicts, and the natural ebbs and flows of life. But how is trust truly built? One of the core elements in any trust-filled friendship is honest communication—speaking with openness and transparency so that both friends feel known and understood.

Yet honesty alone isn't enough. When honesty is wielded without compassion and sensitivity, it can come across as harsh or uncaring, potentially causing harm even when well-intentioned. In friendships, it's essential to balance our honesty with empathy and kindness, ensuring that our words uplift and support rather than wound. This chapter explores how honest communication, when tempered with compassion and sensitivity, becomes a powerful tool for building and deepening trust in friendships.

Honest communication is essential in building trust for any friendship because it establishes a foundation of transparency and authenticity. When friends speak openly, they invite each other into their inner world, sharing their true feelings, thoughts, and concerns. This openness allows both friends to feel seen and understood, which fosters a sense of security. In contrast, friendships built on avoidance or surface-level interactions often lack depth, leaving both people uncertain about where they truly stand.

Honesty in friendship means being willing to communicate not only the good but also the difficult. It involves sharing our true thoughts and feelings, even when they may be uncomfortable. For example, telling a friend how their behavior affected you, even if it risks upsetting them, is a courageous act that strengthens trust. It tells your friend that you value the relationship enough to address issues openly rather than letting resentment build.

In this way, honesty serves as a safeguard against misunderstandings and unresolved issues that can weaken friendships over time.

Trust is reinforced through consistent honesty. Each time friends communicate honestly, they reinforce the message that this is a relationship built on truth, not pretense. This consistency allows both friends to relax. With the knowledge they can rely on each other for genuine responses and that there's no need for second-guessing. As honesty becomes a norm, friends feel more comfortable sharing their true selves, unfiltered and unguarded.

While honesty is essential for building trust, it's crucial to deliver honesty with compassion and sensitivity. These are vital skills to implement in relationships. Raw, untempered honesty can be hurtful, especially when it touches on personal matters. When we speak honestly without considering how our words might affect the other person, we risk causing pain or defensiveness. Compassionate honesty, on the other hand, involves being mindful of how our friend might feel. Striving to communicate in a way that respects their emotions.

Sensitivity in communication means recognizing the nuances of timing, tone, and delivery. For instance, delivering honest feedback when a friend is already feeling vulnerable or stressed can amplify their discomfort. It calls for choosing the right moment, using a tone that conveys care rather than criticism, and finding words that encourage understanding rather than defensiveness.

By approaching honesty with compassion, we show our friends that we care about their feelings and are committed to maintaining a relationship that uplifts them. Compassionate honesty doesn't mean watering down the truth or avoiding difficult topics; it means presenting the truth in a way that is considerate and constructive. This approach deepens trust, as our friends see that we have their best interests at heart and that we're invested in supporting their well-being.

Honesty, when rooted in compassion, strengthens this bond by fostering trust. True honesty in friendship isn't about bluntness or criticism; it's about sharing thoughts and feelings with kindness and care. Compassionate honesty means we're willing to have open, sometimes difficult conversations in a way that uplifts rather than hurts. For instance, if a friend is making decisions that seem harmful, honest compassion might involve gently expressing concern rather than ignoring the issue or being harsh. This balance of truth and kindness allows friendships to grow deeper, creating a foundation where both friends feel safe to be authentic, knowing they are seen, heard, and cared for. Together, compassion and honesty transform friendships into enduring connections where both people can thrive authentically.

Honesty, in all its forms, is the bedrock upon which trust is built. A great friend does not sugarcoat the truth or shy away from difficult conversations. They speak their truth with kindness and respect, knowing that honesty is not just about telling it like it is, but about offering it with the intention of helping the other person grow.

Being honest in a friendship doesn't mean being blunt to the point of harshness; it means speaking with integrity, even when the words are difficult to say. It means offering constructive feedback, having uncomfortable conversations, and knowing when to tell your friend something they might not want to hear—because, ultimately, you want what's best for them.

Honesty also means being open about your own feelings and vulnerabilities. It's about being able to say "I don't know" or "I need help" when that is the truth. In a friendship, honesty isn't just a one-way street, it's a reciprocal exchange of openness that strengthens the bond between friends.

Truth is the backbone of any lasting friendship, but it doesn't mean being blunt or hurtful. True honesty in friendship comes with kindness, patience, and timing. It's about caring enough to speak the truth, not to wound, but to help. Being honest doesn't mean saying everything that comes to mind; it means saying what matters, in a way your friend can receive. Kind honesty respects the other person's feelings while staying true to your own. It's the gentle but clear reminder when a friend is slipping into something that might hurt them, or the encouragement they didn't know they needed, even if it's a little uncomfortable to say.

I've found that some of the most meaningful moments in friendship come when someone cares enough to be real with you. I once had a friend who noticed I was constantly putting myself last, burning out while trying to keep everything together. One day, she said, "I love how much you give, but I worry you're forgetting to take care of yourself." It caught me off guard, but the way she said it with no judgment, just quiet concern made it stick. That kind of honesty opened my eyes, not only to my own habits, but to the depth of our friendship. It taught me that when honesty comes from love, it doesn't push people away, it brings them closer.

Effective Solutions to Communicate Honestly with Compassion and Sensitivity

There are effective solutions to balance between honesty and compassion. Striking the right balance requires practice and self-awareness. Here are some effective solutions to help communicate honestly while showing sensitivity and compassion:

1. **Choose the Right Timing**: Timing is crucial in delivering honest feedback. Before speaking, consider whether your friend is in the right state of mind to receive it. If they are already dealing with stress or emotional turmoil, it might be more compassionate to wait for a calmer moment.

2. **Use "I" Statements**: When sharing honest feedback, use "I" statements rather than "you" statements. This approach frames your feedback as your personal experience rather than an accusation. For example, saying, "I felt hurt when…" instead of "You hurt me by…" reduces defensiveness and invites understanding.

3. **Express Empathy**: Acknowledge your friend's perspective before sharing your own. Saying something like, "I understand that you've been going through a lot lately, and I appreciate your efforts..." shows empathy and sets a compassionate tone for the conversation.

4. **Focus on Specific Behaviors, Not Character**: When giving honest feedback, address specific behaviors rather than making general statements about your friend's character. For example, instead of saying, "You're always inconsiderate," say, "I felt disappointed when you didn't follow through on our plans last time." This approach makes it easier for your friend to understand without feeling attacked.

5. **Be Open to Their Perspective**: Honest communication is a two-way street. After sharing your thoughts, invite your friend to share theirs as well. This openness fosters mutual respect and understanding, showing that you value their perspective as much as your own.

Rachel and Emily had been friends since childhood, but over time, Rachel had become more withdrawn, spending less time with Emily and not sharing much about what was going on in her life. Emily began to notice that Rachel seemed unhappy but didn't know what to say. One day, after weeks of feeling confused, Emily gently approached Rachel and asked, "Is everything okay? I feel like you've been pulling away, and I'm worried."

Rachel initially hesitated, but then, after a pause, opened up about struggles she had been facing in her personal life; issues with a relationship, a difficult work environment, and a growing sense of isolation. Emily, though surprised, thanked Rachel for trusting her and offered a listening ear. Emily's honesty in addressing the situation was the turning point Rachel needed to open up about her struggles.

Friendships built on compassionate honesty tend to be stronger and more resilient. These traits have a long-term impact on our relationships. When friends feel that they can communicate openly without fear of harsh judgment or defensiveness, they are more likely to address issues as they arise rather than letting them fester. This openness prevents small misunderstandings from growing into larger conflicts. It helps both friends feel comfortable expressing their needs and concerns.

Over time, compassionate honesty also deepens mutual respect. When friends are consistent in approaching each other with sensitivity and empathy, they demonstrate that they value each other's feelings and well-being. This respect creates a strong bond that is difficult to break, even when challenges arise. In fact, the willingness to communicate honestly and compassionately during difficult moments can make the friendship even more resilient, as both friends see that they can rely on each other for support and understanding.

Moreover, compassionate honesty encourages personal growth. Friends who communicate openly and constructively help each other become better versions of themselves. Honest feedback, delivered with care, allows us to see our blind spots and make positive changes. This growth oriented approach benefits both individuals, as each friend feels supported in their journey of self-improvement.

Compassion and honesty are pillars of meaningful friendship. It allows us to see our friends' struggles and joys through a lens of empathy. Supporting them in a way that is sensitive to their unique experiences. When we approach our friends with compassion, we offer understanding without judgment, creating a safe space where they feel valued and accepted. This consideration makes us more patient and forgiving. Knowing that just as we have our own imperfections and challenges, so do our friends.

Strategies for Navigating Difficult Conversations

Difficult conversations are inevitable in any close friendship, but they don't have to be destructive. Navigating these necessary talks is easier when approached with compassionate honesty. These conversations can strengthen the friendship by clearing up misunderstandings and reinforcing trust. Here are some strategies for navigating difficult conversations with grace and respect:

1. **Set a Positive Intention**: Before starting a difficult conversation, take a moment to clarify your intentions. Approach the conversation with the goal of understanding and resolving the issue, rather than "winning" or proving a point. Setting a positive intention creates a more collaborative atmosphere.

2. **Listen Actively**: Active listening is essential during difficult conversations. Give your friend space to share their perspective, and make an effort to truly understand their feelings. Reflect back what you hear, showing that you're fully engaged and committed to finding a resolution.

3. **Acknowledge Their Feelings**: Even if you disagree with your friend's perspective, acknowledge their feelings. Statements like, "I can see that this really hurt you, and I'm sorry for any role I played in that" demonstrate empathy and validate their experience.

4. **Stay Calm and Centered**: Emotions can run high during difficult conversations. Difficult conversations can trigger strong emotions, particularly when discussing sensitive topics or past hurts.

Another effective strategy is to take a few deep breaths before responding. Allowing yourself a moment to collect your thoughts. This pause can prevent impulsive reactions and give you the space to approach the conversation with patience and clarity. If you find yourself becoming overwhelmed or emotionally charged, consider taking a short break. Explain to your friend that you need a moment to gather your thoughts and you will return to the conversation when you feel ready to engage with a level-headed perspective.

Staying calm doesn't mean suppressing your feelings; it means expressing them in a way that respects both your own experience and your friend's. A calm and centered approach allows you to address difficult issues without escalating the situation. This approach reinforces to your friend that even during challenging conversations, your commitment to maintaining a respectful, trust-filled friendship remains strong.

The Art of Apologizing and Forgiving in Honest Communication

An often-overlooked aspect of honest, compassionate communication is the willingness to apologize and forgive. In any friendship, mistakes will be made. Even with the best intentions, we may say things that unintentionally hurt or are misunderstood by our friend. When this happens, a sincere apology can go a long way in rebuilding trust.

Apologizing honestly means acknowledging your actions without excuses and expressing genuine remorse. Phrases like, "I'm sorry for how my words made you feel; it wasn't my intention, and I'll try to be more mindful in the future," show accountability and respect. This humility deepens trust, as it demonstrates that you're willing to take responsibility for your actions and prioritize your friend's feelings.

Forgiveness, on the other hand, requires letting go of past hurts and approaching your friend with a renewed sense of trust and openness. This doesn't mean forgetting what happened but choosing not to let past grievances cloud the friendship's future. In healthy friendships based on honest communication and compassion, both apologies and forgiveness become natural parts of the relationship, fostering resilience and understanding. However, we must recognize that some friendships are unhealthy and that is another book altogether.

Continued Legacy

We want to build a legacy of emotional safety and trust in our friendships. When friends practice honest communication tempered with compassion and sensitivity, they create a safe and emotionally nurturing environment. This environment allows each person to express themselves freely, knowing that they'll be met with understanding rather than judgment. As friends consistently communicate with honesty and empathy, they create a friendship that becomes a sanctuary. A place where they can be vulnerable, supported, and authentically themselves.

The legacy of trust built through compassionate honesty has lasting effects. Friends who feel safe sharing their true selves can withstand life's challenges by developing this bond. They are there to celebrate each other's successes, support each other through struggles, and offer constructive feedback that encourages growth. Such friendships enrich our lives, contributing to our emotional well-being and helping us become more empathetic, understanding individuals.

Elliot and Luke had been friends for years, and though they lived far apart, they kept in touch. One winter, when Elliot had lost his job and was feeling particularly down, Luke took it upon himself to show up in a way that only a truly kind friend could. He sent a package with some of Elliot's favorite snacks, a funny book, and a heartfelt note reminding him of his strengths.

Luke knew that what Elliot needed most wasn't grand gestures, but small acts of kindness—reminders that he wasn't alone and that he mattered. Elliot was deeply touched by the thoughtful gesture and found comfort in knowing that his friend cared. It was a simple act, but it reminded Elliot that kindness, no matter how small, can make a world of difference.

Kindness is the smallest yet most profound expression of friendship. It doesn't have to be grand gestures or elaborate displays of affection. Sometimes, kindness is as simple as sending a text to say you're thinking of someone, offering to help with something, or just being there in moments of silence. In its simplest form, kindness is the gentle reminder that the other person matters.

Kindness is also about being patient and forgiving, not just with others, but with yourself. When we offer kindness, we foster an environment where both people can be vulnerable, make mistakes, and grow together. The most powerful friendships are those that are rooted in a kindness that asks for nothing in return—where the act of giving itself is its own reward.

In a world where misunderstandings and superficial interactions are common, friendships rooted in honest, compassionate communication stand out as something extraordinary. They remind us that true connection is built not only on shared experiences but on a foundation of trust, understanding, and mutual respect. By embodying these principles, we can create friendships that are not only fulfilling but deeply meaningful. A true testament to the transformative power of honest, compassionate communication.

In conclusion it is important to base friendships on building trust through honest communication, tempered with compassion and sensitivity. In our journey to become the best friend we can be, practicing this balance of honesty and empathy is a skill that, once mastered, enriches not only our friendships but our own capacity for understanding and love. This will positively affect all of our relationships.

Chapter 4

Respecting Boundaries

Healthy friendships are built on a foundation of mutual respect and understanding, with each person feeling valued, heard, and safe. A core part of this foundation is respecting each other's personal and emotional boundaries. Just as physical boundaries define where we feel safe and comfortable, emotional boundaries protect our inner well-being, setting limits on what feels respectful and appropriate. Recognizing and honoring these boundaries not only maintains harmony in a friendship but also deepens trust and connection.

In friendships, boundaries can range from respecting each other's need for space to honoring personal values and beliefs. We must try to understand the limits of what each person is comfortable sharing or discussing. While each friendship will have its unique dynamic, a commitment to respecting boundaries signals that both friends value each other's individuality and emotional well-being. Let's explore what it means to understand and respect boundaries in friendships and how to navigate these boundaries with care and empathy.

What Are Personal and Emotional Boundaries?

Personal and emotional boundaries are the limits we set for ourselves in relationships to protect our emotional and mental well-being. They define how we wish to be treated, how much we're willing to share, and what we're comfortable with. Emphasizing what is acceptable to us in terms of support, intimacy, and personal space. Boundaries help us feel safe and respected, ensuring that our relationships are nurturing rather than draining or invasive. If relationships are draining, invasive or controlling trust that they are not the nurturing and healthy friendships we are speaking of. This control, invasiveness or draining is not helpful for either person involved in the relationship.

In friendships, boundaries can manifest in many forms such as:

- Time and Space Boundaries: Respecting a friend's need for alone time, downtime, or privacy.
- Emotional Boundaries: Being sensitive to topics that might be painful or uncomfortable for your friend to discuss.
- Communication Boundaries: Understanding how often your friend prefers to communicate and   respecting their preferred modes of communication.
- Support Boundaries: Knowing the limits of emotional support you can provide without overstepping or exhausting yourself.

By setting and respecting boundaries, friends are able to establish clear expectations and avoid misunderstandings. Boundaries aren't walls meant to keep people out; rather, they're guidelines that foster mutual respect and emotional safety. Allowing both people involved to feel safe, respected, and able to grow together.

Why Boundaries Matter in Friendships

Boundaries are essential in friendships because they allow each person to feel secure and autonomous within the relationship. When friends respect each other's boundaries, they demonstrate that they value the other person's well-being and are willing to honor their needs and limits. This mutual respect strengthens trust, as both friends know they can express themselves openly without fear of judgment or pressure.

Boundaries also prevent resentment. In friendships without clear boundaries, one person might feel overwhelmed or uncomfortable, leading to feelings of frustration or even resentment over time. For example, if one friend frequently relies on the other for emotional support but doesn't respect their friend's need for space or personal time, it can create an imbalance in the relationship.
By respecting boundaries, friends avoid these pitfalls, ensuring that the friendship remains a source of joy and support rather than stress or strain.

Furthermore, boundaries encourage healthy individuality. A strong friendship doesn't mean merging identities or always being in sync; it involves two individuals who respect each other's unique perspectives, experiences, and needs. By honoring boundaries, friends create a space where both can grow and thrive as individuals, while still enjoying a meaningful connection.

Boundaries are essential for maintaining a healthy, balanced friendship. They help define the space between individuals and ensure that both parties feel safe, respected, and supported. A great friend understands the importance of personal space and emotional limits. They recognize when to give their friend space to breathe and when to step in with support, all while ensuring their own needs are met as well.

Setting boundaries also means saying "no" when necessary, and not feeling guilty about it. A friendship built on mutual respect and understanding allows both individuals to express their limits without fear of judgment. It's through this mutual respect for boundaries that friends can enjoy the fullness of their connection without it becoming toxic or draining.

Friendship, though built on trust and mutual affection, also requires clear boundaries. It may seem counterintuitive at first; how can boundaries exist in a relationship that thrives on closeness? Yet, boundaries are the very thing that preserve the health of any meaningful relationship, including friendships.

An example of this can be seen in the friendship between Liza and Sarah. Both women were incredibly close, sharing nearly everything with one another. But after years of confiding in each other, Sarah began to feel that Liza was sometimes crossing emotional boundaries by expecting Sarah to always be her emotional caretaker. While Sarah wanted to support her friend, she realized that she was neglecting her own needs in the process.

One evening, Sarah decided to have an honest conversation with Liza. "I love you, and I care about you deeply. But I need to let you know that sometimes, I'm overwhelmed by the emotional demands. I want to be a good friend to you, but I need to find a balance where I can also take care of myself."

Liza was initially hurt, but she appreciated Sarah's honesty. She acknowledged that she had been relying on Sarah too much and agreed to be more mindful of the emotional energy she was requesting. Over time, they learned to navigate their friendship with clearer boundaries, ensuring that both of their needs were being met.

In friendships, as in all relationships, boundaries are not walls to keep people out. They are the spaces that allow us to give of ourselves in healthy, sustainable ways. Without boundaries, friendships risk becoming draining and one-sided, but with them, friendships can flourish. This gives both individuals the freedom to be themselves without resentment.

How to Communicate Boundaries in a Friendship

Communicating boundaries can feel challenging, especially in close friendships, where we might worry about hurting the other person's feelings. However, setting boundaries is a form of honesty and vulnerability that can ultimately strengthen the relationship. The following are some ways to communicate your boundaries and understand those of your friend:

1. **Be Clear and Direct**: While it might be tempting to hint at boundaries indirectly, clear communication is the most effective approach. For example, if you need personal space after a busy week, you might say, "I'm feeling a bit overwhelmed right now and need some downtime. Let's plan to catch up next week." Clear statements prevent misunderstandings and show that you respect both your needs and the friendship.

2. **Express Your Needs as Preferences, Not Ultimatums**: When sharing boundaries, framing them as personal needs rather than demands can make the conversation feel less confrontational. For instance, instead of saying, "You have to stop calling me every day," you could say, "I really value our talks, but I also need some quiet time to recharge. How about we catch up a few times a week?"

3. **Encourage Open Dialogue**: Invite your friend to share their own boundaries and preferences as well. This mutual sharing can deepen trust and help both friends understand each other better. For example, you might say, "I want our friendship to be comfortable for both of us, so please let me know if there are any topics or situations that you're not comfortable with."

4. **Practice Empathy**: If your friend expresses a boundary, practice empathy by acknowledging their feelings and understanding their perspective. Phrases like, "I completely understand; sometimes I need space too," show that you respect their boundary without taking it personally.

5. **Revisit Boundaries as Needed**: Boundaries may shift over time as circumstances change. Check in with your friend periodically to see if their needs have evolved, and share any changes in your own boundaries. This openness keeps the friendship dynamic and responsive to both friends' needs.

Boundaries are essential to our well-being because they protect our mental and emotional health. Fostering balance and mutual respect in relationships. Setting and respecting boundaries allows us to define our limits.
It defines what we're comfortable sharing, giving, or receiving without feeling overwhelmed or resentful. This clarity brings stability, preventing misunderstandings and reducing stress. A welcomed necessity in an overtly invasive, no limits culture we live in.

Respecting Boundaries: Actions That Speak Louder Than Words

Once boundaries have been communicated, respecting them consistently is crucial. Actions demonstrate your commitment to honoring your friend's comfort and well-being. Check out these ways to show respect for boundaries in a friendship:

1. **Honor Time and Space**: If your friend has indicated that they need alone time, respect this by giving them the space they've requested. Avoid interpreting their need for space as a rejection; instead, view it as an act of self-care that ultimately benefits the friendship.

2. **Be Mindful of Sensitive Topics**: If your friend has expressed discomfort with certain topics, avoid bringing them up or pressing for details. Trust that they will share more when and if they're ready. This patience demonstrates respect and builds trust.

3. **Check in Regularly**: Showing genuine interest in how your friend feels about the dynamics of the friendship reinforces that you're committed to a respectful relationship. A simple "Are we good with how we're handling things?" can go a long way in maintaining open communication about boundaries.

4. **Be Patient and Flexible**: Respecting boundaries may require flexibility, especially if your friend's needs differ from your own. For instance, if they need less frequent communication than you, be willing to adjust to a middle ground. Flexibility shows that you value the friendship enough to find a balance that works for both of you.

When boundaries are respected, we feel secure and valued, able to open up and trust without the fear of being judged or drained. In friendships, for instance, boundaries ensure that both people feel heard and supported, allowing each to nurture themselves while contributing to the relationship. Healthy boundaries also empower us to maintain a sense of individuality within our connections. They create a safe space where we can be authentic, knowing our needs and values will be honored. This mutual respect not only enhances emotional well-being but also strengthens the relationship, turning it into a source of renewal and support rather than a drain on our energy.

In this way, boundaries aren't restrictive; they're affirming. By helping us engage meaningfully while protecting our personal well-being, boundaries allow us to build relationships that are both nurturing and resilient.

Lily had always been a compassionate friend, but after a difficult breakup, her friend Jenna became overly reliant on her for emotional support. Jenna would call at all hours of the night, expecting Lily to drop everything to listen to her pain. Lily, though empathetic, began to feel drained and overwhelmed by the constant demands.

After several weeks of feeling mentally exhausted, Lily realized that she needed to set a boundary. With kindness and respect, she gently told Jenna, "I care about you deeply, and I want to support you. But I also need to make sure I'm taking care of myself. I can't always be available at a moment's notice, and I need some space to recharge."

Jenna was initially hurt, but she came to understand that Lily's boundaries were not a rejection, but a way to maintain the health of their friendship. The relationship grew stronger as a result, with both women learning to respect each other's needs.

Respect is not merely about politeness; it's about recognizing and honoring the humanity of the other person. It's about accepting that your friend may have different beliefs, values, or ways of approaching life, and still valuing them for who they are. Respecting your friend means acknowledging their boundaries, honoring their feelings, and giving them the space to be themselves without judgment.

True respect in a friendship means that even in disagreement, there is an underlying understanding that each person's perspective is worthy of consideration. It allows both people to feel safe, heard, and validated, even when they don't always agree. In this way, respect is the scaffolding that allows a friendship to grow and evolve without the risk of one person's needs overshadowing the other's.

Navigating Boundary Crossings with Grace

Even with the best intentions, boundaries can sometimes be crossed, leading to feelings of discomfort or tension. When this happens, addressing the issue calmly and respectfully can prevent further misunderstandings and preserve the friendship. Here's how to navigate situations where boundaries have been unintentionally crossed:

1. **Acknowledge the Boundary**: If your friend communicates that a boundary has been crossed, listen with an open mind. Acknowledge their feelings without becoming defensive. An apology, even if unintentional, shows that you respect their boundary and are willing to make amends.

2. **Take Responsibility**: When boundaries are crossed, it's important to take responsibility for your actions. Express regret and commit to being more mindful in the future. For example, saying, "I'm sorry for overstepping. I didn't realize you needed more space, but I'll respect that going forward," reassures your friend of your intention to honor their needs.

3. **Discuss Solutions Together**: If a boundary crossing has led to tension, collaborate on finding solutions. This might involve adjusting how you communicate or setting clearer guidelines. Working together to address the issue demonstrates mutual respect and a commitment to moving forward constructively.

4. **Practice Forgiveness and Move Forward**: When boundaries are respected, the friendship grows stronger. If both friends are willing to forgive and learn from any boundary crossings, they can move forward with a renewed sense of trust and understanding.

Jesse and Mark had always been close, but when they reached adulthood, they found themselves with differing views on some fundamental issues like politics, lifestyle choices, and even what they wanted out of life. While these differences initially caused some tension, their respect for each other's individuality never wavered.

Instead of forcing their perspectives on one another, they learned to navigate these differences with respect. They listened to each other's points of view, discussed their beliefs calmly, and agreed to disagree when necessary. The respect they had for each other's opinions allowed them to maintain a strong friendship, even when they didn't always see eye to eye.

True Connection

At the heart of all meaningful friendships lies a connection that cannot be quantified by metrics or measured by time spent together. It is a bond that transcends the day-to-day trivialities and instead becomes a deep source of mutual respect, trust, and understanding. It's often in the quietest of moments when you realize how profoundly these relationships shape your life. When a friend's presence is more comforting than words, when their laughter brightens your darkest days, and when their absence leaves an undeniable void in your life.

True friendship isn't about superficial connections, nor is it defined by the number of social media likes or the frequency of meetups. It's about how deeply we care for each other's well-being, how we show up when it matters, and how we remain steadfast through both the easy and difficult times. This kind of bond often begins with small, simple acts, like a thoughtful text when someone is struggling or an unspoken understanding during a moment of silence. These acts slowly accumulate, layer upon layer, until a deep, unshakeable trust is built between friends.

Perhaps the truest example of this is when you experience an overwhelming challenge, one that feels insurmountable. In these moments, you might expect the world to feel heavy, as if the burden is yours alone to carry. But when a friend steps in, without judgment, without hesitation, and simply says, "I'm here, no matter what," it's as if the weight lightens just a little. These friendships become lifelines, threads connecting us to sanity, joy, and the ability to keep moving forward.

In such friendships, the quality of the connection speaks louder than the quantity of interactions. It's the unwavering consistency, even in the face of life's distractions, that turns a mere acquaintance into a lifelong confidant.

Respecting each other's personal and emotional boundaries is a profound way of showing that you care for your friend's well-being. The gift of boundaries is a path to deeper connection. When boundaries are understood and honored, friends feel free to be themselves without fear of judgment or intrusion. Boundaries give each person the space to grow, recharge, and engage with the friendship in a way that feels safe and fulfilling.

Boundaries also foster deeper connections. By respecting a friend's boundaries, you're saying, "I see you, I hear you, and I value what makes you unique." This mutual respect lays the groundwork for a friendship that is both supportive and empowering—a relationship where both friends feel valued as individuals and enriched by the bond they share.
In the end, understanding and respecting boundaries is about building a friendship that honors each person's humanity. It's about recognizing that true closeness comes not from overstepping boundaries but from respecting them. By embracing each other's boundaries, we cultivate friendships that are not only lasting but genuinely nourishing. Where both friends are free to be their fullest, truest selves.

True connection in friendship is rare, powerful, and unmistakably real. It doesn't demand constant validation, nor does it waver in silence. When a friendship is rooted in genuine connection, there is an ease—a natural rhythm in conversation, in presence, and in absence. You feel understood even when your words fall short. Vulnerability isn't met with discomfort or judgment, but with care. Time doesn't corrode it; even distance doesn't dilute it. A true friend won't just celebrate your highs, they'll steady you through your lows, often without needing to be asked.

Signs of True Connection in Friendship:

- **Emotional Safety**: You can be honest without fear. Mistakes, flaws, or fears aren't ammunition—they're bridges.

- **Mutual Effort**: The energy flows both ways. They check in, initiate, remember. You're not the only one trying to keep things alive.

- **Growth-Friendly**: A true friend doesn't keep you small to make themselves feel bigger. They want you to evolve, and they evolve with you.

- **Silence Feels Safe**: You don't always need to talk. Their presence alone is enough.

- **No Transactional Tone**: You're not a favor machine or a means to their ends. The bond is not about what you provide, but who you are.

Recognizing a Fake Friendship:

Sometimes the truth about a friendship arrives quietly—through an unanswered message, a one-sided effort, or a pattern of subtle dismissals. Here are some red flags:

- **One-Sidedness**: You're always the one reaching out, apologizing, or adjusting. If you're bending until you break, it's not mutual.

- **Conditional Presence**: They show up when it's convenient for them—or when they need something. Your crisis feels like a burden, theirs is a headline.

- **Jealousy or Competition**: Your wins make them distant, not delighted. Instead of cheering, they compare.

- **Gossip and Disloyalty**: If they speak ill of others to you, expect they'll speak ill of you to others. A friend who gossips is a friend in costume.

- **Inconsistent Values**: If you're constantly compromising your dignity or principles to keep the peace, it's not a real connection—it's survival.

Constant proof is not required in true friendship, it proves itself quietly over time. Fake friendships often ask for your loyalty while offering none in return. Trust your body: if you leave interactions feeling drained, small, or unseen, it's not a home—it's a warning.

And remember: the right people never need to be chased. Real friendship walks beside you. We have to recognize when to walk away.

Fake friends wear the mask of loyalty but disappear when it no longer benefits them. They celebrate your failures more than your wins, take more than they give, and drain your spirit with subtle disloyalty or indifference. You'll notice the conversations revolve around them, your value is tied to what you can offer, and your presence feels optional. Walk away when your peace is disturbed more than protected, when you're shrinking to stay connected, or when your trust begins to feel like a burden. Real friendship, as in all real relationships, doesn't ask you to question your worth.

Chapter 5

Thoughtful Acts of Kindness

Friendship is woven from countless little moments that, over time, create a deep and meaningful connection. While grand gestures may occasionally play a part, it's often the small, thoughtful acts that create lasting memories, cementing the bonds that make friendships truly special. Thoughtful acts remind us that we are seen, valued, and appreciated. These acts, whether as simple as a heartfelt message or as elaborate as a well-planned celebration, can bring a sense of joy, comfort, and support that lingers long after the moment has passed.

In the busyness of life, it's easy to take friendships for granted. We assume that our friends know we care, or that time together alone will suffice to maintain the connection. Yet thoughtful kind acts hold a special power in friendships. They are a tangible way to show that we pay attention, that we remember, and that we prioritize each other's happiness. Kind acts that remind our friends that they matter deeply to us. Let's delve into how these thoughtful acts enrich friendships, creating memories and reinforcing bonds in ways that make a lasting impact.

The Power of Attention: Thoughtfulness in Everyday Moments

Thoughtful gestures don't have to be grand or elaborate. In fact, some of the most memorable gestures are small but deeply personal, often stemming from a keen awareness of what matters to our friends. It could be as simple as sending a text when you know your friend has a big day, or offering them a favorite snack during a study session because you know it comforts them. These gestures may seem minor, but they carry weight because they show that you're paying attention to the details of their life and personality.

Imagine a friend who remembers your quirks and preferences—a particular author you admire, a tea flavor you always order, a song that reminds you of home. When they acknowledge these details in their actions, it becomes clear that they're truly attuned to who you are. Thoughtful gestures like these affirm our uniqueness, making us feel appreciated for the specific individuals we are. In a world where we often feel rushed or unnoticed, having a friend who takes the time to truly see us is invaluable.

One example of this could be a friend remembering an upcoming event that's important to you. Perhaps you mentioned in passing that you have a job interview or a family gathering you're feeling anxious about. A simple message wishing you luck or checking in afterwards can mean the world, showing that they're with you in spirit even if they can't be there in person. These small acts show a friend's care in a way that words alone might not, reminding you that you're not facing life's ups and downs alone.
Creating Shared Joy Through Meaningful Surprises

One of the most delightful aspects of friendship is the joy of surprising each other. Surprises don't always need to be extravagant; even a small, unexpected gesture can create a ripple of happiness that lasts. These gestures are rooted in the knowledge of what would bring joy to your friend—a favorite book they mentioned wanting to read, a coffee on a particularly stressful day, or a playlist of songs they love.

Meaningful surprises are about going beyond convenience to show that you've thought about what might brighten your friend's day. This could be arranging a group video call if they've been feeling lonely, or decorating their desk at work to celebrate a promotion. These surprises create shared memories, experiences that both friends can look back on and remember as moments of genuine joy and connection. The element of surprise adds a layer of excitement, a small thrill that reinforces the bond and makes both friends feel like they're actively creating happiness together.

It's also worth noting that surprises in friendship don't have to happen on special occasions. Some of the most meaningful surprises come simply "because." A spontaneous road trip, an unexpected handwritten letter, or a dinner prepared just because they've had a hard week. These surprises speak to the strength of the friendship. They signal that you don't need a holiday or a milestone to show your friend you care; your bond is reason enough.

To show your friends kind gestures doesn't have to be grand or expensive. Sometimes often the smallest gestures that mean the most. A simple message asking how your friend is doing, showing up when they need someone to talk to, or even remembering their favorite coffee order can make a big difference. These little actions show that you care, that you're paying attention, and that your friend matters to you. Taking the time to celebrate their achievements, support them during tough times, or just being present in their life consistently is what helps friendships grow stronger over time.

I remember a time when my best friend was going through a really stressful period during final exams. She was feeling overwhelmed and hadn't been sleeping well. One day, without saying anything, I showed up at her house with her favorite chocolate milk and a handwritten note that simply said, "You've got this. I believe in you." We didn't even talk for long, but I could see how much it meant to her. Later, she told me that moment gave her the motivation to push through. It wasn't a big gesture, but it reminded both of us how powerful small acts of kindness can be when they come from the heart.

Tough Times

We can show support to our friends through small acts of kindness during tough times.
True friends stand by us not only in celebration but also in our most challenging moments. During tough times, small, thoughtful acts of kindness can be especially powerful. While grand gestures of support are appreciated, sometimes it's the quiet, steady presence and the small acts of kindness that mean the most. When a friend is going through a difficult period, thoughtful actions like checking in regularly, bringing over a meal, or

simply sitting with them in silence can provide comfort in a way that words cannot.

Consider a friend who's recently experienced a loss or disappointment. They might not want to talk about it, and they may even withdraw for a time. A thoughtful gesture in this situation could be as simple as sending a message that says, "I'm here whenever you need, no pressure." Or perhaps dropping off a book or a candle with a note that says, "Just something to let you know you're not alone." These acts allow you to be there for them without overwhelming them, offering support that is gentle but deeply meaningful.

In tough times, thoughtful gestures tell our friends that they don't have to carry their burdens alone. It's a way of holding space for them, letting them know that no matter what they're going through, someone is there to walk alongside them.
These gestures are not about solving their problems. They are about reassuring them that they're loved and supported, exactly as they are, no matter what they're facing.

As friendships grow over the years, the memories we create together become a cherished part of the relationship. Thoughtful acts of kindness are often the catalyst for these memories, serving as touchpoints that remind us of the depth of the friendship. Whether it's a small tradition like an annual coffee date or a surprise birthday celebration. These gestures become moments we can revisit time and time again, bringing back the joy, warmth, and closeness of the friendship.

For example, two friends might have a tradition of writing each other letters on New Year's Eve, reflecting on the past year and setting intentions for the next. These letters become a keepsake, something they can look back on and smile about as the years go by. Or perhaps one friend has a habit of bringing flowers on the first day of spring, marking the start of a new season together. These memories become part of the fabric of the friendship, small threads that weave together to form a rich tapestry of shared experience.

Thoughtful gestures also serve as milestones that commemorate the evolution of friendship. As time passes, friends change and grow. But the gestures they've shared over the years serve as a reminder of the love and care that has remained constant. The shared memories aren't just sentimental. They are evidence of the commitment and effort that both friends have put into nurturing their connection.

Kindness in friendship isn't always about big, dramatic actions. Often it is found in the little things that show someone genuinely cares. For me, one of the kindest things a friend has ever done is send me encouraging texts every single week. No matter how busy life got, they would always take a moment to check in and send a few words that lifted my spirits. Sometimes it was a simple "you've got this," and other times it was a longer message reminding me of how far I've come. It didn't take much time, but it made a huge difference. Those messages reminded me that I wasn't alone and that someone believed in me, even when I was struggling to believe in myself. That kind of consistent kindness is quiet but powerful. This is what makes a friendship truly special.

Traditions

In friendships, traditions can be a powerful way to reinforce bonds. A thoughtful act of kindness can become a special tradition. Something that friends look forward to and that strengthens the friendship each time it's repeated. These traditions don't have to be elaborate or expensive; in fact, the most meaningful customs are often simple acts that carry deep personal significance.

For instance, perhaps two friends have a tradition of watching a particular movie every year on their shared birthday month. Or they have a habit of exchanging homemade gifts during the holidays. These customs become something both friends can count on, a reminder that their friendship is a consistent and valued part of each other's lives. These traditions create continuity and give the friendship a sense of stability, even as other aspects of life change.

Traditions can also be adapted to fit different stages of life. Friends who once spent hours together every week might now be separated by distance or busier schedules. A weekly phone call, a shared playlist, or even a postcard tradition can become a thoughtful custom that keeps the friendship alive across distances and through time.

Thoughtful gestures, whether big or small, remind us that friendship is an active, living relationship that requires care, attention, and love. These acts of kindness create moments of happiness, memories to cherish, and traditions that add meaning and stability to our lives. In a world where time and energy are limited, thoughtful acts communicate that we prioritize our friendships. Telling each other that we value them enough to make time and put in effort to show our appreciation.

These acts aren't about grandiosity; they're about consistency, sincerity, and attention to detail. Through thoughtful gestures, we create friendships that are resilient and fulfilling. We remind our friends and ourselves that true friendship is a gift. One that deserves to be nurtured and celebrated.

Ultimately, thoughtful gestures are a language of love and care in friendships. They're the everyday expressions of appreciation that say, "I value you, I see you, and I'm here for you." When we make the effort to be thoughtful, we honor the connection we share with our friends, creating a legacy of memories and moments that will stay with us long after the gestures themselves are over. It is these acts of , big and small, that turn friendships into lifelong sources of joy, strength, and comfort.

Creating Lasting Memories Through Small, Thoughtful Gestures

1. **Reach Out with Regular Check-Ins:** A quick message or call to see how your friend is doing shows you're thinking of them. Even a simple

"Hope your day is going well" can brighten their day and remind them that you care.

2. **Remember Special Dates and Milestones**: Acknowledging birthdays, anniversaries, or personal achievements demonstrates that you're invested in their life. A small "Thinking of you on your big day" text or a card on their work anniversary can mean a lot.

3. **Show Appreciation with Simple Acts of Kindness:** Actions like grabbing their favorite coffee or sharing a thoughtful compliment create small moments of joy. These gestures don't have to be grand; it's the intention that matters.

4. **Send Encouraging Notes or Messages:** A spontaneous text like "You've got this!" before a big meeting or exam shows that you remember and believe in them. Such small affirmations make them feel supported and understood.

5. **Listen Attentively and Reflect on Past Conversations:** Recalling and asking about details they've shared in past conversations, like a project they were working on or a family event, demonstrates that you listen closely and value what they have to say.

6. **Share Meaningful Content:** Sending a book recommendation, article, or meme that reminds you of them or aligns with their interests shows that you're thinking of them in a personal way and strengthens shared interests.

7. **Offer Support in Day-to-Day Life:** Helping out with small tasks, like giving them a ride or running an errand, communicates reliability. These everyday acts show that you're there for them, not just in special moments but in the fabric of daily life.

8. **Celebrate Their Everyday Wins:** Acknowledge their smaller accomplishments—like finishing a difficult week or successfully tackling a

new hobby. Saying "I'm proud of you" for small victories shows you recognize and value all aspects of their journey.

9. **Plan a Surprise Celebration:** Organizing a celebration for a friend's big achievement or special occasion creates a memorable experience. Whether it's a small gathering or a surprise party, the effort shows you're invested in marking their milestones.

10. **Create a Personalized Gift:** Thoughtful, personalized gifts—like a photo album, scrapbook, or a handmade item that reflects shared memories—create lasting memories and deepen the bond. Personalization shows that you put effort into creating something meaningful.

11. **Organize a Fun Day or Adventure Together:** Plan an outing that aligns with their interests, such as a day trip, hiking adventure, or a visit to a museum they love. Shared experiences create cherished memories that reinforce the friendship.

12. **Be There for Major Life Events:** Showing up for big moments, such as weddings, graduations, or family gatherings, demonstrates unwavering support. Your presence during these times becomes a lasting reminder that you're a part of their most important memories.

13. **Offer Your Time During Difficult Moments:** Being there physically and emotionally during tough times—like the loss of a loved one, job struggles, or personal setbacks—can be a profound gesture. Providing a supportive presence during life's hardships strengthens the friendship deeply.

14. **Celebrate Shared Achievements and Milestones Together:** If you and your friend have shared milestones, like reaching fitness goals or finishing a project together, take time to celebrate them as a team. This not only celebrates individual growth but reinforces the friendship's shared journey.

15. **Give Them a Thoughtful, In-Person Goodbye or Welcome**: When they're moving or returning from a significant trip, organizing a send-off or a welcome-back celebration shows your commitment to supporting them during transitions and making them feel cherished.

16. **Make a "Just Because" Gesture that Reflects Their Passions:** Thoughtful "just because" gestures—like arranging a cooking class if they love cooking, or buying concert tickets for their favorite band—show that you understand their passions and want to be a part of their joys.

These steps give ideas on how both small, consistent gestures and bigger, more significant acts can create meaningful memories and reinforce the foundation of a lasting friendship. Through a mix of everyday support and thoughtful celebrations, friends can continuously strengthen their connection.

Kindness in true friendship and relationships is rarely about grand declarations—it lives in the quiet, consistent gestures that say, *"I see you."* A thoughtful message on a hard day, remembering a small detail from a past conversation, showing up without being asked. These are the threads that weave trust and intimacy. It's the way someone pours your tea without asking how you take it, because they already know. Small acts don't just support a relationship, they sustain it. In a world that often rushes past connection, kindness slows down, anchors us, and reminds us that being loved doesn't always come in loud ways. It often comes in the gentle, ordinary moments that feel like home.

Simple kindness from friends shown through traditions and thoughtful gestures:

- A friend who texts you every morning before a big meeting or exam just to say, *"You've got this."*

- One who remembers the anniversary of your loss and quietly checks in, offering space to talk or just sit with you.

- Friends who host a "just because" dinner each month where everyone brings something homemade, honoring your tradition of gathering and sharing life.

- A friend who keeps a playlist of songs that remind them of your friendship and shares it on days you need encouragement.

- Someone who surprises you with a small item you mentioned weeks ago in passing—a book, a snack, or a quote they knew you'd love.

- A yearly tradition of sending holiday ornaments with a personal note about what they appreciated about you that year.

- A friend who waits with you at the doctor's office, even if it means rearranging their day.

- One who frames a photo from a meaningful trip or moment and gives it to you "just because."

- Friends who make it a point to celebrate even your smallest wins—a job interview, a finished project, or just getting through a tough day.

Friendship often shows itself through meaningful traditions and quiet, thoughtful gestures that speak louder than words. A friend who always sends a handwritten note on your birthday, no matter the distance. One who brings your favorite comfort food after a tough week without being asked. A yearly tradition of watching the same movie together during the holidays, just because it matters to you both. A friend who saves little mementos from shared moments—a concert ticket, a photo strip—because they value your time together. These acts may seem small, but they're the heartbeat of true friendship: consistent, personal, and rooted in care.

Chapter 6

Celebrating Success Supporting Failures

Friendship finds some of its deepest roots in the shared experiences of joy and adversity. As we journey through life, the highs and lows we face can feel either amplified or softened by the people we have beside us. True friendships aren't just about spending time together or sharing common interests; they are about lifting each other up in moments of triumph and standing as pillars of support when things become difficult. There's a special joy in celebrating a friend's achievements as if they were our own, and there's an unspoken strength in knowing we can be each other's refuge when life presents challenges.

In this chapter, we will explore how friendships flourish when we become each other's cheerleaders and anchors, and how these roles, though different, are equally essential to a lasting, fulfilling bond. Through acts of celebration and support, friends can show that they are truly invested in each other's lives, standing as living testaments to the power of shared joy and resilience.

One of the most beautiful aspects of friendship is the ability to celebrate each other's achievements with genuine joy and pride. The power of shared joy. It takes a particular kind of person to see another's success as a reason for personal happiness. Someone who isn't focused on comparison or competition but is wholeheartedly invested in the well-being of their friend. When we celebrate our friends' milestones, we acknowledge their hard work, their struggles, and their triumphs. These celebrations, whether big or small, become moments of shared joy that reinforce the bond between us.

Celebrating our friends' achievements doesn't always mean hosting a grand event or planning an elaborate surprise. It can be as simple as sending a congratulatory message, taking them out for coffee to commemorate the occasion, or expressing our pride through a heartfelt compliment. The key to it is sincerity. When our friends know we're genuinely happy for their success, they feel valued and supported. This is particularly meaningful because achievements, though rewarding, can sometimes feel isolating or overwhelming. By joining in the celebration, we make our friends feel less alone in their success. Reminding them that their joy is our joy too.

For instance, a friend who lands a new job may be excited but also anxious about the change. A thoughtful celebration, like surprising them with a "new beginnings" gift or taking them out to toast to their success, can transform their apprehension into enthusiasm. Showing them that they have a support system that believes in their ability to thrive. In moments like these, friends become more than just companions. They become our cheerleaders, the ones who see our potential and are proud of us every step of the way.

Milestones

Life is full of milestones. Graduations, promotions, weddings, and other major achievements that signify personal growth and progress. As friends we should honor each other's milestones and big life achievements. When friends make an effort to honor these occasions, it strengthens the friendship and builds a foundation of support and encouragement. Celebrating milestones together becomes part of the shared history that bonds friends, turning life's big moments into memories that both can cherish for years to come.

Imagine a friend who goes above and beyond to celebrate your wedding anniversary, a graduation, or a career milestone. These moments mark major transitions, and by being there, they are affirming that they see and respect your growth. These celebrations go beyond surface-level acknowledgment; they recognize the journey, the hard work, and the sacrifices that have led to that moment. When friends make these efforts, they send a message that they're not just along for the ride. But they are invested in our journey and in seeing us succeed.

Honoring milestones also means adapting to the different seasons of each other's lives. Friends might be in different stages. One may be getting married while another is pursuing a career change, or one might be having a child while another is going back to school. Instead of comparing or drifting apart, true friends find ways to celebrate each other's unique paths. They create an environment where every milestone, no matter how different from their own experiences, is celebrated with enthusiasm and respect. In doing so, they enrich their friendship and build a lasting bond of mutual support and pride.

Acknowledging small everyday victories is important. While milestones hold great significance, everyday achievements deserve celebration too. Life isn't solely defined by major events; it's composed of countless small victories that contribute to our growth and well-being.
Recognizing these everyday wins in our friends' lives can be incredibly meaningful. It shows that we're paying attention not just to the highlights but to the little moments that make up their daily lives.

For example, a friend who has successfully made it through a particularly challenging week at work deserves acknowledgment, even if it doesn't seem like a "big" accomplishment. A simple message like, "I'm proud of you for pushing through" or a spontaneous coffee date to decompress can mean a lot. These small gestures tell our friends that we see their efforts, that we're proud of their resilience, and that we're with them every step of the way. Recognizing these smaller victories can create a habit of celebration within the friendship. Turning each little triumph into a shared moment of happiness.

Moreover, celebrating everyday victories reinforces positivity within the friendship. It reminds both friends that life's journey isn't just about reaching major milestones; it's about appreciating the little moments of growth and success that make each day worthwhile. By cultivating this attitude of recognition and encouragement, friends build a relationship that is consistently uplifting. Where both feel appreciated for their efforts and are motivated to continue pushing forward.

Celebrating achievements is a joyful aspect of friendship, but perhaps even more profound is the role friends play in supporting each other through difficult times. Being a source of strength and standing together through challenges display genuineness in relationships. Life isn't always easy, and at some point, everyone faces challenges. Whether it's personal loss, professional setbacks, health issues, or emotional struggles. In these moments, the presence and support of a friend can make all the difference. A true friend is one who stands by us in adversity, providing comfort, understanding and reassurance that we're not alone.

True friendship isn't just about showing up for the victories, it's about standing beside each other in both the triumphs and the defeats. Celebrating success feels even sweeter when you share it with someone who's seen the full journey, from uncertain beginnings to hard-earned wins. But real connection deepens when you can also bring your failures into the light, knowing you won't be judged, only supported. I remember a time when I landed a position I'd worked so hard for, and my friend surprised me with a homemade dinner and a tiny card that simply said, "Told you so." It was heartfelt, personal, and full of kindness. That same friend was also there months later when I faced a setback that shook my confidence. There were no grand gestures, just a quiet presence, a listening ear, and a reminder that failure wasn't the end, just part of the story. Those shared moments, both the highs and the lows, are what built the kind of friendship that lasts. One that is rooted in unconditional support and mutual growth.

Supporting a friend during tough times isn't always about finding solutions or offering advice. Often, it's simply about being there. Sometimes, the most comforting thing we can do is to sit with a friend in silence, allowing them to feel whatever they need to feel without judgment. Being a source of strength means creating a safe space where they can express their emotions freely, without fear of being misunderstood or dismissed. It's about offering a shoulder to lean on, a listening ear, and a reminder that they are loved, no matter what.

For instance, when a friend experiences the loss of a loved one, they may feel a range of emotions, from sadness to anger to guilt. In this vulnerable state, having a friend who is willing to listen without judgment. One who checks in regularly, or who offers a small act of kindness like a home-cooked meal, a handwritten note, or simply a warm embrace, can provide immense comfort. These gestures, though seemingly small, communicate a powerful message: "I'm here for you, no matter what."

Encouragement

During challenging times, friends often need encouragement and reassurance that things will eventually get better. While we can't predict or control what happens in life, we can remind our friends of their own strength and resilience. Encouragement from a friend can be incredibly powerful because it comes from someone who knows us well, someone who has witnessed our journey and believes in our ability to overcome. Encouragement can take many forms: a reminder of past challenges they've successfully navigated, words of affirmation that recognize their courage and determination, or simply a gentle nudge to take things one day at a time. For a friend going through a job loss, for example, a message that says, "I believe in you, and I know you'll find something even better," can make a significant impact. It's not about empty words; it's about genuinely believing in their potential and reminding them of their own inner strength.
Reassurance also means normalizing difficult emotions and validating their experience. Friends can offer a unique perspective, one that acknowledges the pain while also providing a sense of hope. A friend who says, "It's okay to feel this way; you're going through a tough time, and it's normal to struggle" can make their friend feel understood and less isolated. By providing reassurance, friends help each other navigate life's challenges with a sense of hope and resilience.

Strengthening the Bond Through Mutual Support

The beauty of friendship lies in its reciprocity. Both friends take on the role of celebrator and supporter, creating a relationship that is balanced and fulfilling. When we celebrate each other's achievements, we add joy to our lives; when we support each other through hardship, we build trust and resilience. Over time, these moments of shared joy and strength become the foundation of a lasting friendship, one that is defined by mutual respect, care, and loyalty.

Being both a source of joy and strength for each other means that the friendship becomes a safe haven, a place where both friends can turn for support, encouragement, and celebration. This mutual support creates a bond that is not only resilient but deeply fulfilling, as both friends know they have someone who will stand by them no matter what. This balance of celebrating the good times and weathering the tough times is what makes friendship so profound; it's a relationship that enriches our lives, adding depth, joy, and strength to each step of our journey.

In the end, the joy of celebrating each other's achievements and being a source of strength during tough times is what makes friendship one of the most valuable relationships we can have. These moments, big and small, are the essence of true friendship.

They are the reminders that, through the ups and downs of life, we have someone who will cheer us on, lift us up, and walk alongside us, come what may.
In a world that can sometimes feel isolating, this companionship, this shared joy and resilience, is a precious gift that adds immeasurable value to our lives.

Celebrating Each Other's Achievements

1. **Express Genuine Enthusiasm:** When your friend achieves something, show sincere excitement and pride. Congratulate them warmly, whether in

person or through a thoughtful message, and let them know that their success brings you joy.

2. **Acknowledge Their Hard Work and Effort**: Recognize the effort and dedication your friend put into reaching their achievement. Acknowledge their journey by saying something like, "I know how hard you worked for this—congratulations!"

3. **Celebrate in a Way That Aligns with Their Personality:** Tailor the celebration to fit your friend's style. If they love gatherings, throw a small party; if they're more low-key, a thoughtful gift or coffee date might be just right. Consider what would make them feel genuinely appreciated.

4. **Capture the Memory:** Take photos, write a card, or save mementos from the celebration. Small keepsakes can remind both of you of this shared joy and will serve as a cherished memory that reinforces your friendship.

5.**Encourage Them for Future Goals:** After celebrating, let your friend know you believe in their future potential. Words like "I can't wait to see what you accomplish next!" show that you support them beyond this single achievement.

6. **Reflect Their Happiness Back to Them:** Sometimes people feel a mix of pride and modesty about their achievements. Reflect their happiness back, helping them feel good about celebrating themselves, which adds to their sense of pride and joy in the moment.

7. **Involve Their Support Network if Appropriate:** If it feels right, include others in their support circle—friends, family, or colleagues who may also want to celebrate. This can amplify the experience and reinforce how valued they are by the people around them.

Being a Source of Strength During Tough Times

1. **Offer Your Presence and Listen Actively:** Sometimes, just being there is enough. Let your friend know they're not alone, and listen to them fully without interrupting or immediately offering advice. Give them a space to express their feelings openly.

2. **Reassure Them of Your Support:** Verbally reassure your friend by saying things like, "I'm here for you" or "You don't have to go through this alone." Knowing they have a supportive friend can make a world of difference in difficult times.

3. **Respect Their Coping Process**: Each person copes differently. Some may want to talk, while others may need space. Respect their approach and avoid pushing them to cope in a specific way, even if it differs from your own preferences.

4. **Offer Practical Help:** In tough times, daily tasks can feel overwhelming. Offer tangible support, like helping with errands, cooking a meal, or assisting with responsibilities. Practical support can ease their burden and show your care in action.

5. **Check In Regularly Without Being Overbearing:** Consistent, gentle check-ins remind your friend that you're there for them over time. A quick message saying, "Thinking of you—let me know if there's anything you need" can show support without overwhelming them.

6. **Help Them Find Perspective When They're Ready:** When the time feels right, gently help them see things from a balanced perspective. Avoid minimizing their feelings, but remind them of their strengths and past resilience, offering hope for getting through the current situation.
7. **Encourage Self-Care and Healthy Coping Strategies:** Gently remind your friend of the importance of self-care during challenging times. Encouraging them to rest, eat well, and practice self-compassion can help them stay grounded, even in the midst of adversity.

8. Celebrate Small Wins in Their Healing Process: Recovery can be slow and challenging, but celebrating small steps—like getting through a difficult day or making progress in a difficult task—can lift their spirits. Show that you notice and are proud of their resilience.

In real friendship, it's not just about cheering during the highs, but quietly standing by during the lows. I've learned that sometimes the most meaningful support isn't loud or dramatic, it's simply knowing when to show up and when to give space. One of my closest friends and I have always had this unspoken understanding. When I got accepted into a competitive program I'd worked tirelessly for, they didn't flood me with messages or post anything online. They just called, said "I knew you could do it," and took me out for ice cream. Simple, but unforgettable. And when things didn't go so well , like the time I poured everything into a project that flopped, I wasn't rushed with advice or forced positivity. Instead, I received a text, "Whenever you're ready to talk, I'm here." That message said everything. It reminded me that support doesn't always have to be loud or constant to be powerful. Sometimes, just letting someone know you're there, no pressure, no judgment. is the greatest act of kindness you can offer in a friendship.

These are great ways to provide a thoughtful approach to both celebrating achievements and being a source of strength during hard times. Nurturing a balanced and supportive friendship built on shared joy and unwavering support.

Chapter 7

Regular Check-Ins

Maintaining a meaningful connection with a friend isn't just about grand gestures or extraordinary events. It's about the ongoing dedication to staying engaged through consistent communication and presence. In friendships, as with any significant relationship, connection is built over time, layered by moments of shared laughter, understanding, and support. In the modern world, staying close requires conscious effort and understanding of each other's needs. Especially when life can be demanding and time-consuming. This section looks into the heart of staying connected through consistent communication and presence. Exploring how simple, yet intentional acts help create and sustain a powerful, lasting friendship.

Consistent communication in friendship plays an important role. At its core, friendship thrives on connection, and connection is often rooted in communication. Maintaining this communication keeps the channels open between friends. It helps them navigate each other's lives, celebrate successes, and be present for one another during challenges. Even in friendships where daily interaction isn't necessary, finding a rhythm that works for both parties is key.

In modern friendships, communication can take many forms: text messages, phone calls, video chats, and face-to-face conversations. The medium may change, but the importance lies in the regularity and quality of these exchanges. Studies show that even small touchpoints, such as a "thinking of you" message, can significantly strengthen bonds between people. Such gestures are simple but convey that a friend is actively in your thoughts and that you care about their day-to-day life. It's this ongoing sense of engagement that keeps a friendship feeling vibrant and alive. Different friendships thrive on different frequencies and rhythms of communication. For some, daily contact feels natural and necessary, while others maintain a close connection with weekly or even monthly check-ins. To maintain a healthy friendship, it's essential to establish and respect this rhythm. Ensuring that both friends feel heard and understood. A conversation about communication preferences can be valuable. This conversation might include questions like:

- How often do you like to talk or catch up?
- Do you prefer texting, calling, or meeting in person?
- How do you feel about spontaneous calls or messages?

By aligning expectations, friends can find a balance that suits both parties, reducing the likelihood of misunderstandings or feelings of neglect. This rhythm doesn't have to be rigid. Life circumstances change, and communication needs may vary. Still, having an understanding of each other's preferences goes a long way in ensuring that both friends feel valued.

Real friendships don't have to follow a strict timeline. They ebb and flow with life's seasons, yet remain steady at their core. I have a friend like that. We don't talk every day, or even every week. Sometimes months go by, and once, almost a year passed without communicating. But somehow, without fail, one of us will send that familiar message: *"Hey, just thinking about you. How's your heart?"* It's never awkward, never forced. We pick up exactly where we left off, as if time had politely stepped aside for us. These check-ins have become our quiet tradition. A reminder that friendship doesn't have to be loud or constant to be real. Sometimes it's a five-minute voice note in the middle of a chaotic week. Other times it's a long catch-up over coffee when schedules finally align. But it's always sincere. What makes it special is the mutual understanding: we may drift, but we never disappear. That kind of friendship, built on respect and quiet consistency, has taught me that showing up doesn't always mean being present every day. It means being present when it matters, in a way that never lets the other person feel forgotten.
"Micro-Moments"

Not all communication needs to be lengthy or in-depth. Micro-moments are short, meaningful interactions often just as impactful as extended conversations. A quick message, a funny meme, or a photo that reminds you of your friend can be a great way to stay connected without the need for an elaborate check-in. These micro-moments are low-effort, high-reward actions that remind your friend they're in your thoughts, even on a busy day.

For instance, sharing something that made you think of them, or sending a simple "Good luck today!" before their big meeting can make a significant difference. These gestures are small, but they show thoughtfulness, which adds up over time. A friendship built on consistent small interactions can feel stronger and more connected than one that only includes occasional in-depth exchanges. The idea here is that presence can be felt even in a few seconds. This reinforces a friend's value in your life.

Open and authentic communication is another pillar of sustained engagement in friendships. Friends should feel free to express their thoughts, emotions, and needs without fear of judgment. This openness isn't only about sharing problems. It's also about sharing joys, dreams, fears, and hopes. When friends communicate honestly, they build a foundation of trust that enables them to grow closer over time.

However, open communication also means being considerate and respectful. Knowing when to listen and when to offer advice is crucial. Sometimes, friends just need a sounding board. They may not want solutions but instead desire empathy and understanding. Being a good listener is often more valuable than being a problem solver.

Presence in friendship goes beyond physical proximity. In many cases, a friend's presence can be felt deeply even from miles away. It's about showing up mentally and emotionally, not just physically. Presence is a testament to a friend's commitment and care, and it makes a profound difference, especially during both high and low points in life.

One of the most tangible ways to demonstrate presence is by showing up for significant events in a friend's life. Whether it's a graduation, wedding, or family gathering, being there for these major life moments reinforces a friend's sense of support and belonging. These events provide the opportunity to celebrate each other's achievements, milestones, and transitions.

However, it's equally important to be there for the quiet, everyday moments. Being present doesn't always mean being there for the big, obvious occasions; sometimes, it's about being there for no reason at all. The moments spent in each other's company, without any special occasion, are just as significant. These experiences create the kind of comfort and familiarity that make a friendship feel like home.

Emotional Presence

Emotional presence is about more than just physical presence; it's about being in tune with a friend's emotional state and responding appropriately. Emotional availability means being ready to offer empathy, understanding, and encouragement whenever a friend needs it. This can be as simple as offering a listening ear during a difficult time or sending a supportive message when a friend is feeling low.
When a friend shares a vulnerability, it's essential to acknowledge it with respect and compassion. These moments of vulnerability deepen trust and allow friends to grow closer. Emotional availability means creating a safe space where both friends feel free to share without fear of being dismissed or judged.

Quality Time

Quality time is essential in a friendship, as it strengthens the bond through shared experiences and mutual enjoyment. In today's busy world, carving out time for friends can be challenging, but prioritizing this time demonstrates a commitment to the relationship. Whether it's a regular coffee date, a monthly outing, or even just a shared hobby, spending time together in person fosters a deeper sense of connection.

Even virtual interactions can serve as quality time when physical presence isn't possible. For friends separated by distance, video calls, online games, or virtual movie nights provide ways to engage meaningfully despite the miles. These activities show that distance doesn't have to diminish the connection when both friends are committed to staying present.

A strong friendship doesn't require constant communication; instead, it respects each other's independence while maintaining a reliable connection. Balancing independence with consistent engagement allows both friends to grow individually and as a unit, bringing fresh perspectives and experiences into the friendship.

Embracing Each Other's Unique Needs

Personal growth can sometimes change the dynamics of a friendship, as each person's life experiences and perspectives evolve. Embracing this growth means respecting and encouraging each other's personal journeys, even if they lead down different paths. When friends allow each other to pursue new interests, goals, and relationships, they bring renewed depth and insight into the friendship.

For example, if a friend pursues a new career, relationship, or passion, the other friend can support them by staying engaged, asking questions, and showing curiosity. This creates a friendship where change is welcomed, not feared. When friends feel free to grow without risking their bond, they are more likely to stay connected and committed over time.
Consistent connection doesn't mean overbearing contact. In fact, respecting each other's need for space can strengthen the friendship. There will be times when a friend may need to focus on personal issues or self-reflection, and understanding this need without taking it personally is vital. Giving space when necessary allows both friends to recharge and come back to the friendship with renewed energy and appreciation.

Recognizing when space is needed requires sensitivity and intuition. By being attuned with each other's moods and life situations, friends can support each other in the most helpful ways, whether by providing company or giving room for solitude. This ebb and flow create a rhythm
that is both respectful and resilient.

Balancing Communication and Presence

Friendship, like any relationship, requires nurturing. It's not the grand gestures alone that solidify the bond but the consistent acts of care, thoughtfulness, and connection that make a friendship endure. By fostering open, honest communication, being present for both the highs and lows, and balancing connection with independence, friends create a foundation that can withstand the
test of time.
In a world where distractions are constant and life's demands can feel overwhelming, making time for friends is a powerful act of loyalty and love. This consistent engagement reminds each friend that they have someone who values, supports, and cherishes them, creating a friendship that becomes a source of joy, strength, and companionship.

As we've discussed, constant contact isn't always necessary, we can move with the rhythm of life, sometimes quiet, sometimes close, but always present in a meaningful way. Joe and Silas are that kind of pair. They've been friends for years, yet their conversations don't follow a schedule. Sometimes they'll talk every few weeks, sometimes it's months, or years. But eventually, one of them will reach out with a simple message: *"You crossed my mind today. How's life?"* There's no guilt, no pressure, just an honest check-in that says, "I'm still here."

Their friendship is rooted in something deeper than frequency. When Joe landed a new job, Silas didn't flood him with congratulations, he sent a short voice message saying, "Proud of you, man. Let's catch up soon." And when Silas was going through a rough patch, Joe didn't push for details. He just texted, "Take your time. I'm around when you're ready." It's this mutual respect for space, mixed with a steady commitment to showing up, that has kept their bond strong over time. Joe and Silas may not speak every day, but in a world full of noise, their quiet, dependable friendship speaks volumes.

It's easy to get caught up in the busyness of life, letting days slip into weeks and months without reaching out. But friendships, even the strongest ones, need care. Sometimes just a small reminder that someone is thinking of you. Like Joe and Silas, we don't always need to talk every day to keep a connection alive. A simple message, a short call, or even just a shared memory sent out of the blue can make all the difference. So remember to check in with your friends. Not because you have to, but because it matters. That small act might be exactly what they need. It's a quiet way of saying, "I'm still here, and I still care."

Maintaining consistent communication and presence may take effort, but it's this very effort that transforms friendships into some of the most fulfilling relationships we can have in life.

Chapter 8

Handling Conflicts with Grace

In any relationship, friendships included, conflicts are inevitable. Differences in perspective, values, and experiences often lead to moments of disagreement or tension. Yet, instead of viewing conflict as something to avoid, we can embrace it as an opportunity for growth and deeper understanding. When approached with openness, respect, and maturity, conflicts in friendship can lead to stronger, more resilient bonds. Addressing differences constructively reveals insights into each other's needs, preferences, and boundaries, which are vital for a lasting connection. This section delves into how to navigate conflict in friendships in ways that foster growth, mutual respect, and a stronger foundation of trust.

A Natural Aspect of Friendship

Conflict is often seen as negative, but in reality, it's a natural part of any close relationship. In friendships, conflicts arise from honest expressions of individual needs and boundaries. These tensions don't have to weaken a friendship; rather, they can strengthen it when both friends are willing to engage openly and respectfully. Often, what drives conflict is not a lack of love or care but simply different interpretations or expectations.

When we accept that conflict is inevitable, we begin to see it less as a threat and more as an opportunity. Friends who work through conflicts are more likely to understand each other on a deeper level, as these moments of tension prompt important conversations. These conversations can bring clarity to unspoken needs or previously misunderstood behaviors. In this way, conflict becomes a tool for personal growth within the friendship. inviting both individuals to communicate more effectively and empathize with each other's perspectives.

Changing Perspective: View Conflict as Growth-Focused

A growth-focused approach to conflict shifts the mindset from "winning" or "losing" an argument to focusing on mutual understanding and learning. Rather than viewing disagreements as disruptions, friends who adopt this mindset recognize that working through issues together can lead to a more satisfying and resilient friendship. Instead of fearing that a disagreement will drive a wedge between them, they see it as an opportunity to strengthen their connection.

This perspective doesn't deny the discomfort that comes with conflict. Addressing a sensitive issue with a friend can feel daunting, especially when emotions are high. However, by staying open to the idea that these challenges are ultimately constructive, friends can approach conflict with a sense of purpose and shared commitment.

Friendship is not without its challenges. But with grace, which is the ability to forgive, to accept imperfections, and to give second chances, we are ensured that those challenges don't break our friendship bonds. Grace is the quiet strength that says, "We all make mistakes, but we can learn and grow from them." It is the forgiveness that allows for healing, the understanding that no one is perfect, and the ability to extend compassion even when things go awry.

A great friend does not hold grudges; instead, they offer grace, knowing that the friendship is worth more than any misstep or disagreement. They understand that mistakes are part of being human, and they are willing to move past them, knowing that the heart of the friendship is still intact. Grace is a refreshing part of friendship. You will find when you extend this refreshing you will yourself feel refreshed.

Emotional Intelligence in Conflict is Important

Navigating conflict requires a level of emotional intelligence. The ability to recognize, understand, and manage our own emotions while empathizing with those of others. Emotional intelligence helps friends approach conflict with calm and consideration. Allowing them to communicate without escalating tension or being offended. By being aware of one's emotional triggers and responses, a person can engage in difficult conversations with greater self-control and understanding. Remembering our friends honor us by sharing their deep emotions with us. Connecting on this kind of intimate level.

Emotional intelligence also means recognizing that, during conflict, emotions are a natural part of the process. Anger, frustration, or sadness may arise, but they do not have to define the conversation. Friends who handle conflict maturely acknowledge their feelings without allowing those feelings to lead to hurtful behavior. They strive to separate emotion from action, focusing instead on expressing their feelings constructively.

Openness in conflict means being willing to share your own perspective honestly while also being receptive to your friend's viewpoint. It involves clear, honest communication and a willingness to listen without defensiveness. When friends are open during disagreements, they create a safe space for each other to express thoughts and feelings. This leads to greater mutual understanding.

Practicing Transparency and Honesty

One of the most important aspects of openness is transparency. When conflicts arise, it's essential to communicate one's thoughts and feelings openly. If, for example, you feel hurt by something your friend said, expressing this directly and honestly can prevent resentment from building up. Starting with "I feel" statements like, "I felt overlooked when…" or "I felt misunderstood when…", helps keep the focus on your emotions rather than assigning blame. This approach can soften the conversation and open a door to understanding. It allows the other person to hear your feelings without feeling attacked.

Honesty also means owning up to one's own role in the conflict. This can be challenging, as it requires vulnerability. But when friends are honest about their own mistakes or misunderstandings, they show humility and a willingness to grow. Admitting a misstep or misunderstanding can be as simple as saying, "I realize now that I might have misinterpreted what you meant," or "I didn't realize how my words affected you." Such admissions are acts of strength, not weakness, and they encourage the other person to respond with equal openness.

Cultivating Active Listening

Active listening is a fundamental part of openness in conflict resolution. It's easy to assume that we already understand our friend's perspective, but active listening requires us to put aside assumptions and genuinely focus on what the other person is saying. This means not just hearing the words but also paying attention to tone, body language, and emotional cues.

When friends practice active listening, they show that they value each other's thoughts and feelings, even when they don't fully agree. Phrases like "I hear you" or "I understand that this is important to you" convey validation, which can defuse tension. Paraphrasing what the other person has said such as, "So, you're feeling hurt because I...", can also clarify their perspective and prevent misunderstandings. Active listening allows both friends to feel heard and understood, which is often more important than reaching an immediate resolution.

Respect is essential in any relationship, especially during moments of tension. When friends approach conflict with respect, they communicate a commitment to preserving the friendship and valuing each other as individuals, even amid disagreement. Respect means recognizing each other's perspectives, speaking kindly, and showing empathy. This prevents conflicts from becoming toxic or damaging.

Avoiding Assumptions and Judgments

Respectful conflict resolution involves avoiding assumptions and judgments about the other person's intentions or character. It's common, especially in the heat of the moment, to assume the worst: "They don't care about my feelings," or "They're being selfish." These assumptions often distort the reality of the situation, leading to unnecessary escalation.

Instead, approach conflict with curiosity rather than judgment. Ask questions to clarify your friend's perspective and express a willingness to understand their motivations. For example, you might say, "I felt hurt when this happened, but I want to understand why you said that," rather than jumping to conclusions. This approach shows respect for your friend's experience and makes it easier to find common ground.

However, if these instances are recurrent and difficult to resolve, you must ask yourself if the relationship is genuine from both sides. Be careful to recognize toxicity in unrecognized mutual responsibility in the relationship.

Avoiding Blame and Using "I" Statements

Placing blame is a common response in conflict, but it rarely leads to resolution. Statements that begin with "You always..." or "You never..." are often perceived as attacks. This can lead the other person to respond defensively. Instead, focusing on "I" statements keeps the conversation centered on one's own experience, reducing the likelihood of defensiveness.

For example, rather than saying, "You never listen to me," you could say, "I feel unheard when I'm interrupted." This rephrasing shifts the focus to your own feelings, making it less accusatory. This respectful approach enables the other person to respond without feeling attacked, encouraging a more collaborative resolution process. Again, recognizing the willingness of both parties in the relationship to assume proper responsibility for their own actions.

Showing Empathy and Understanding

Empathy is one of the most powerful tools in conflict resolution. By putting oneself in the other person's shoes, a friend can better understand why they acted or reacted in a particular way. Empathy doesn't require complete agreement with the other person's viewpoint.It simply requires a willingness to see the situation from their perspective.

During a conflict, showing empathy might mean acknowledging the other person's emotions with statements like, "I can see that this is really important to you," or "I understand why you might feel that way." By validating their emotions, friends show that they care about each other's feelings, making it easier to reach a place of mutual respect and understanding.

Maturity in conflict resolution involves self-awareness, patience, and a focus on long-term friendship health over immediate emotional gratification. It means managing emotions, accepting responsibility for one's actions, and working toward constructive solutions rather than dwelling on grievances. This refers to both of you and should not constantly be a one-sided venture.

Taking Time to Reflect Before Reacting

In moments of conflict, emotions can cloud judgment and lead to impulsive reactions. Taking time to pause, breathe, and reflect before responding allows friends to approach the situation with a clearer mind. This pause helps prevent regretful words or actions and ensures that both individuals can engage in a thoughtful conversation.

Pausing doesn't mean avoiding the conflict. Instead, it's an opportunity to gather thoughts and consider one's true feelings. Sometimes, stepping back can reveal that the initial reaction may not fully represent the underlying issue. With a bit of distance, friends can approach the conversation with greater clarity and a willingness to listen.

This is an important precursor allowing our personal reactions to subside so that we can have a better perspective. Giving us each a chance to think thoroughly before responding emotionally or from any hidden triggers. Reflection from this vantage point helps us avoid unnecessary damage to our relationship. Ultimately fostering growth for everyone involved.
Taking Responsibility

In any conflict, both parties contribute to the dynamic in some way. Taking responsibility for one's own actions and reactions is a sign of maturity and integrity. Rather than focusing solely on what the other person did wrong, mature friends acknowledge their role in the situation. This can involve admitting when they overreacted, misunderstood, or failed to communicate effectively.

Taking responsibility might look like saying, "I realize that I could have handled that better," or "I didn't mean to come across as dismissive." Such admissions don't erase the other person's role but demonstrate accountability. These statements encourage a collaborative rather than adversarial resolution.

Solutions Over Grievances

Mature conflict resolution involves shifting the focus from grievances to solutions. Instead of rehashing every detail of the disagreement, friends who prioritize solutions work together to find a path forward. This could involve discussing how to avoid similar conflicts in the future or establishing clear boundaries to prevent misunderstandings.

By focusing on solutions, friends demonstrate that their primary concern is the health of the friendship, not "winning" the argument. In healthy relationships it is not about 'winning' or 'losing'. This forward-thinking approach allows both parties to leave the conversation feeling heard, respected, and optimistic about their continued connection. Allowing stronger bonds to be built.

Carlos and Jake had been friends for many years, but Carlos made a mistake that threatened to sour their relationship. He had accidentally shared a personal secret of Jake's with someone else, and it hurt Jake deeply. When Carlos realized the impact of his mistake, he was overwhelmed with guilt and fear that their friendship was over.

But when Jake confronted him, he didn't react with anger or bitterness. Instead, he acknowledged that he had been hurt but also recognized that Carlos was genuinely sorry. With grace, Jake forgave him and assured him that while the breach of trust would take time to repair, he valued their friendship enough to move forward. Carlos was humbled by Jake's grace and resolved to be more careful in the future.

Strength comes with Constructive Conflict

Conflict in friendship is not an end but an opportunity for growth, understanding, and deeper connection. When approached with openness, respect, and maturity, conflicts can reveal the values, needs, and boundaries that each person holds dear. By embracing these moments of tension with a commitment to friendship, friends create a stronger foundation based on mutual respect, empathy, and honesty.

Safe, constructive conflict in a relationship is not a sign of failure, it's a sign of maturity. It means both people feel secure enough to be honest, even when the truth is uncomfortable. In healthy conflict, the goal isn't to win, but to understand. Voices may rise, but respect never falls. There's space for emotion without fear of retaliation, and disagreement doesn't threaten the bond, it deepens it. When handled with care, conflict becomes a bridge, not a barrier. It shows that love isn't about avoiding tension, but about choosing each other through it.

In navigating conflict constructively, friends learn more about each other, communicate more effectively, and ultimately grow together. Instead of fearing conflict, they can view it as an invitation to build a friendship that is resilient, compassionate, and enriching. A friendship where both individuals are empowered to be their true selves. This is growth.

Chapter 9

Apologies and Forgiveness

In every friendship, mistakes and misunderstandings are bound to occur. Even the best of friends may occasionally say something hurtful, make an assumption, or fail to be there when they're needed most. What matters in these moments is how we navigate the aftermath; how we approach the mistake, seek to understand its impact, and extend forgiveness. When handled with care, mistakes and misunderstandings can actually bring friends closer. They can reinforce trust and resilience in the relationship. Let's look at the significance of genuine apologies and forgiveness. And some practical steps to help friends mend and strengthen their bond after a misstep.

Making mistakes is part of being human. In friendships, errors can sometimes hurt feelings or strain the connection. But know they also present an opportunity to grow, learning more about each other's needs and values. Misunderstandings or mistakes can clarify expectations, reveal unspoken boundaries, and encourage friends to communicate more clearly. These natural truths often illuminate the areas where we're still learning how to care for each other in the best way possible.

A friendship that has never been tested by a mistake or misunderstanding may lack depth. It's through navigating these challenges that friends truly understand the strength of their bond. When a friendship can endure moments of tension and emerge intact, it becomes more resilient and meaningful. Achieving this resilience requires that both friends approach mistakes with humility, honesty, and a willingness to make amends.

Genuine Apologies

A sincere apology is the cornerstone of healing after a mistake. Apologies that are genuine acknowledge the hurt caused, demonstrate empathy, and convey a commitment to avoid repeating the same error. Offering a genuine apology requires vulnerability. It means taking responsibility for one's actions without shifting blame or minimizing the impact. We must take ownership of our mistakes.

To offer a genuine apology, it's essential first to recognize the impact of your actions on the other person. This means empathizing with their feelings and understanding the extent of the hurt caused. For instance, if a friend feels neglected or dismissed, acknowledging their experience without trying to downplay it is crucial. Saying something like, "I understand that my words came across as dismissive, and I can see why that hurt you," shows that you value their feelings and are willing to see things from their perspective.

By validating their emotions, you demonstrate that you're not just apologizing to "move on," but are genuinely invested in repairing the relationship. When friends feel that their pain is acknowledged, they're more likely to open up, which sets the stage for a deeper and more healing conversation. This allows for more meaningful connection.

Defensiveness and Blame Shifting

One of the biggest obstacles to a genuine apology is defensiveness. When we feel that our character is being questioned, it's natural to want to defend ourselves. But doing so often minimizes the other person's experience. Defensiveness, even if unintended, can send the message that we're more concerned with protecting our ego than with understanding the hurt we caused. It is important to acknowledge our friends' pain in order to be genuine.

For an apology to be sincere, it's important to set aside defensiveness and focus instead on the other person's perspective. This may involve recognizing that, while our intentions may not have been to cause harm, the impact was nonetheless painful. Avoiding phrases like, "I'm sorry you feel that way," which can come off as dismissive. Opt for statements that take ownership, such as, "I'm sorry for my actions, and I understand that they caused you pain," this reflects a mature and responsible approach.

Accountability

Regret is a key component of any heartfelt apology. By expressing regret, you're communicating that you understand the impact of your actions and wish you had acted differently. Accountability is equally important; it means taking full ownership of your role in the situation without any justifications.

A genuine apology might sound like, "I'm really sorry for not being there for you when you needed me. I realize now that my absence made you feel unsupported, and I wish I had shown up for you in that moment". This type of apology not only acknowledges the impact but also conveys a commitment to making things right.

One of the most difficult, but necessary, aspects of being a great friend is the ability to apologize. Apologizing isn't about admitting defeat or weakness; it's about owning your mistakes, taking responsibility for your actions, and showing the courage to make things right. An apology isn't just about saying "I'm sorry", it's about understanding the hurt you've caused, expressing genuine remorse, and taking steps to do better in the future.

A great friend knows that the act of apologizing strengthens the bond between them and their friend. It shows maturity, accountability, and a deep care for the relationship. The willingness to apologize is not a sign of weakness but a sign of strength. It takes great humility to acknowledge when we've been wrong and to work toward repairing the damage.

In many ways, forgiveness is the quiet foundation on which enduring friendships are built. It is not always easy to forgive, especially when we feel deeply hurt by those we love most. But the ability to forgive is one of the greatest gifts we can offer in a friendship.

Take the story of Clara and Emma. Clara had always been fiercely protective of Emma, but one day, Emma made a decision that hurt Clara deeply. She had unknowingly crossed a boundary, taking a private conversation Clara had shared in confidence and spreading it among mutual friends. Clara was devastated, feeling betrayed by someone she trusted so much.

For weeks, Clara struggled with anger, disappointment, and hurt. But she also recognized that holding onto these emotions would only poison the relationship they had built over years. One evening, after much contemplation, Clara reached out to Emma. "I've been angry, and I'm still hurt by what happened. But I want you to know that I'm ready to move forward, if you're willing to own what happened and make things right."

Emma, feeling the weight of her actions, apologized sincerely, acknowledging how deeply she had hurt Clara and explaining that it was never her intention to betray that trust. In that moment, Clara realized that forgiveness was not about erasing the past, but about choosing to release the hold it had on her and move forward, even when it was difficult. Clara forgave Emma, not for her sake alone, but for the sake of their friendship. Through this process of forgiveness their bond deepened, not because the pain had been forgotten, but because they had chosen to learn and grow from it

Real Change

An apology is just words unless it's backed up by action. True accountability involves committing to change and demonstrating through future behavior that you're serious about not repeating the mistake. Friends who apologize sincerely also take steps to prevent similar misunderstandings or hurts in the future. This commitment might mean setting reminders, establishing better communication practices, or checking in more regularly.

Real dedication in this manner is truly enlightening to many areas of our lives and all relationships. Enabling growth on multiple levels to sustain positive practices through accountability. This is the kind of friend we want and want to be.

An example, if a friend often feels unheard during conversations, you could commit to practicing active listening. This shows them that you value their perspective. When friends see that you're willing to make changes to prioritize their needs, it reassures them that the apology is authentic. A good step to build trust that the same issue won't continue to arise.

Forgiveness is as much a gift to oneself as it is to the other person. Holding onto resentment or hurt can weigh heavily on a friendship, while choosing to forgive opens the door for healing and a fresh start. Forgiving doesn't mean forgetting or excusing the hurt; rather, it's about acknowledging the pain, accepting the apology, and deciding to move forward without holding a grudge.

Sophie and Hannah had been inseparable for years, but a misunderstanding during a trip had caused a rift between them. Sophie had accused Hannah of betraying her, and Hannah had responded defensively, pushing Sophie away. They didn't speak for months, each holding on to their own hurt.

One day, Sophie realized that the years of friendship they shared meant more than the misunderstanding that had come between them. She reached out to Hannah, offering an apology for the part she had played in their fallout. Hannah, in turn, forgave Sophie, acknowledging that they both had misinterpreted each other's actions.

Through forgiveness, they rebuilt their friendship, learning that true friendship can survive even the deepest hurts when both people are willing to let go of past grievances and make room for healing.

What Forgiveness Means

Forgiveness in friendship means choosing to let go of resentment and consciously deciding to rebuild trust. It's about moving beyond the mistake and allowing the friendship to grow without constantly revisiting the past hurt. Forgiveness requires patience and understanding. Rebuilding trust may take time, especially if the hurt was significant.

Forgiveness also involves setting boundaries if necessary to protect one's well-being. If a friend repeatedly crosses a boundary, forgiving them doesn't mean ignoring the issue. It means having an honest discussion about expectations to ensure both friends feel respected moving forward. Not immediate retrust. This is a process to rebuild.

Forgiving a friend can have profound emotional benefits, both for the relationship and the individual. Holding anger or resentment can create a barrier that stifles connection, making it difficult to feel close or trusting. By choosing to forgive, friends create space for empathy and understanding, which often strengthens their bond.

Forgiveness also fosters personal growth. Learning to forgive enables individuals to develop greater emotional resilience, empathy, and compassion. Friends who practice forgiveness are often more capable of handling future challenges together. Knowing that their bond can withstand difficult moments.

Forgiving doesn't always happen instantly. Depending on the severity of the hurt, it may take time to process emotions and feel ready to forgive. Patience and communication are essential here; it's okay to communicate that you're still working through your feelings and need time to reach a place of forgiveness. True forgiveness is authentic and not rushed, so allowing yourself the time to forgive fully will make the act more meaningful and lasting.

Ideas for navigating mistakes and misunderstandings in friendships:

1. **Acknowledge the Mistake Without Defensiveness**: Begin by recognizing the mistake openly and without defensiveness. Set aside any urge to explain or justify, and simply accept that your actions caused harm.

2. **Listen Actively to Understand the Impact**: Give your friend the space to express their feelings and listen with an open mind. Avoid interrupting or interjecting; let them share their perspective fully before responding.

3. **Express Empathy and Acknowledge Their Feelings**: Show that you understand their hurt and genuinely empathize with their experience. Use phrases like, "I can see why that would hurt," to validate their emotions.

4. **Apologize Sincerely and Take Responsibility**: Offer a heartfelt apology that takes full responsibility for your actions. Avoid blame-shifting language and focus on owning your role in the situation.

5. **Commit to Preventing Future Misunderstandings**: Take actionable steps to prevent the mistake from happening again. This could mean communicating more openly, respecting boundaries, or setting reminders for important commitments.

6. **Give Your Friend Space if Needed**: Sometimes, after an apology, the other person may need time to process. Respect their need for space and avoid pressuring them to forgive immediately.

7. **Embrace Forgiveness to Rebuild Trust**: Once your friend is ready, work together to forgive and rebuild trust. Understand that trust restoration is a process, and be patient and consistent in showing up for each other.

8. **Move Forward Together, Focused on Growth**: Rather than revisiting the past hurt repeatedly, focus on the lessons learned and the ways you can strengthen your friendship moving forward.
Tessa and Naomi had been best friends for years, but during a heated argument, Tessa said something that she deeply regretted. The words she had spoken were hurtful and untrue, and she knew that no matter how the conversation had unfolded, her words had caused damage.

After some time had passed, Tessa took it upon herself to apologize. She called Naomi and said, "I need to apologize for what I said. I spoke out of anger and frustration, and I deeply regret hurting you. What I said wasn't true, and I take full responsibility for my words. I value our friendship too much to let this go unresolved."

Naomi, though hurt, appreciated the sincerity of Tessa's apology. Tessa's ability to take responsibility for her actions and offer a heartfelt apology was the first step toward healing the rift between them.

A Path to Stronger Friendships Through Mistakes and Forgiveness

Navigating misunderstandings with genuine apologies and forgiveness is one of the most powerful ways to cultivate resilient, meaningful friendships. These moments of vulnerability, humility, and empathy allow friends to see each other's humanity and strengthen the foundation of their connection. Through heartfelt apologies, committed change, and patient forgiveness, friends can transcend their mistakes or misunderstandings, transforming them into opportunities for growth and a deeper bond.

True friendships are not defined by the absence of conflict but by the willingness to navigate challenges with respect, understanding, and compassion. Each time friends work through a mistake or misunderstanding together, they reaffirm their commitment to the relationship. This creates a friendship that is capable of withstanding life's inevitable ups and downs. By embracing both the power of genuine apologies and the gift of forgiveness, friends can build a lasting connection that continues to grow, evolve, and enrich both their lives.

At our core we long for stronger connections, this is a vital aspect of our make up. Remembering in the human condition that not one of us is perfect. We will have to navigate the ups and downs of life including but not limited to mistakes and forgiveness of thus. As we desire the same treatment when we commit these inescapable errors.

Chapter 10

Encouraging Growth and Positivity

In an ideal friendship, both people act as champions for each other's growth. Nurturing each other's dreams and goals with unwavering optimism and encouragement. When friends genuinely support each other's ambitions and growth, they create a relationship that fosters mutual inspiration, joy, and resilience. Such friendships offer a safe space where friends can explore their passions, take risks, and pursue goals with the assurance that someone truly believes in them.

Let's talk about how to build a friendship that not only accommodates personal growth but actively supports it. Inspiring each friend to become the best version of themselves. We'll look at the importance of optimism, positivity, and intentional encouragement.Including some steps to help both friends thrive within a relationship that feels like a partnership in growth.

A Culture of Encouragement

Supporting each other's growth starts with creating a foundation of encouragement. A supportive friendship acknowledges the importance of each person's unique goals and aspirations. Nurturing these dreams with enthusiasm and positivity. This culture of encouragement involves celebrating wins, offering a shoulder during setbacks, and believing in each other's potential even in the face of challenges.

It's essential that each friend feels their goals and dreams are valued and taken seriously. Regardless of how different they might be from each other's own ambitions. A culture of encouragement also promotes vulnerability, where friends can share their fears, setbacks, and ambitions without fear of judgment or dismissal.
A positive, growth-oriented friendship is marked by genuine excitement for each other's successes. Celebrating these moments, no matter how big or

small, reinforces that both people are invested in each other's journey. These celebrations might look like congratulating a friend on a work promotion, recognizing their effort in a challenging personal project, or even supporting them as they take small steps toward a long-term dream.

Celebrating success also means avoiding envy or competition. Instead, it's about viewing each other's achievements as a shared joy, acknowledging that one person's growth doesn't diminish the other's. This dynamic builds a powerful sense of partnership. Each person will know they have someone cheering for them wholeheartedly.

Friendships, like people, evolve. They grow with us, adapt to our changing needs, and withstand the pressures that life places on them. A true, lasting friendship is one that endures not because it is static, but because it is capable of change.

Consider the journey of Frank and Natalie. They had been friends since high school, but as they entered adulthood, their paths began to diverge. Frank married and settled into a stable family life, while Natalie pursued her career with vigor, moving from city to city, constantly on the move. For a while, their friendship was strained by distance, and the sense of ease that had once existed between them was replaced by a quiet tension, as if they had grown too different to maintain the bond.

But one evening, when Natalie returned to town for a visit, she and Frank sat down for a long conversation about their lives, where they had been and where they were going. In that conversation, they realized that while their lifestyles had changed. However the core of their friendship, the trust, the shared memories, and the understanding of each other's true selves, remained intact.

Frank and Natalie did not attempt to return their friendship to what it had once been. Instead, they found a new rhythm, one that acknowledged their differences and respected their individual paths. They learned that friendships can evolve, and in doing so, they become even more meaningful. The bond they shared was no longer defined by proximity or common experiences, but by the enduring mutual respect and love they had for one another.

Safe Spaces

Growth inevitably comes with challenges, and a supportive friendship serves as a sanctuary where both people can share their struggles without fear of judgment. This safe space allows friends to be honest about setbacks, doubts, or failures, knowing they won't be met with criticism or dismissal.

A friend who truly supports personal growth will listen compassionately, provide validation, and remind the other of their strengths. Rather than offering unsolicited advice or quick fixes, this type of friend simply holds space. Allowing their friend to feel seen and understood. By offering this non-judgmental support, friends create an environment where growth can flourish, even in the face of difficulty.

True friendship, as we have seen in these stories, often reveals itself most profoundly through vulnerability. It is not in the masks we wear to protect ourselves from the world, nor in the idealized versions of ourselves that we present to others. Instead, it is in the moments when we allow ourselves to be truly seen. For someone to see the raw, unfiltered versions of ourselves. That is when the most meaningful connections are forged.

Consider the story of Mia and Olivia. Mia had always been the one to take care of others, always strong, always dependable, always looking out for those around her. But after years of carrying the weight of everyone else's expectations; Mia found herself exhausted, both physically and emotionally. She had reached a breaking point and was unsure of how to proceed. For the first time in her life, she felt like she couldn't be strong anymore.

When Mia confided in Olivia, she did so with trepidation, afraid that her admission of vulnerability might change how Olivia saw her. But Olivia's response was not judgment but a quiet, steady support. "You've been there for me through so much, Mia. You don't have to be strong all the time. It's okay to not have it all together," she said.

That simple acceptance, that permission to be imperfect, shifted something in Mia. It was then that she realized that true friendship doesn't require us to be unbreakable, untouchable, or without flaw. Instead, friendship thrives on mutual vulnerability, the willingness to reveal our fears, our doubts, and our brokenness. When we are able to lean on our friends in our most fragile moments, we discover the depth of trust and love that can exist between two people.

Authenticity and Self-Discovery

Friendships that support personal growth encourage authenticity. This allows both people to pursue their goals without feeling pressured to conform or compromise. A friend who truly supports your growth celebrates your individuality, encouraging you to stay true to your values, interests, and passions. Even when they may differ from their own.

Every person's journey is unique, and a supportive friendship respects and embraces these differences. Rather than trying to mold each other into a particular image or ideal, friends who foster
personal growth celebrate what makes each person unique. This means encouraging each other to pursue goals that resonate on a personal level. Especially if they're unconventional or challenging.

When friends embrace originality, they provide the kind of support that feels empowering rather than limiting. This openness to originality allows each person to explore their full potential without feeling pressured to fit a particular mold or meet expectations that aren't their own. In a culture where there can be a lack of uniqueness lets embolden our friends' originality.

Growth

A growth-oriented friendship encourages self-reflection, allowing both friends to explore who they are. Friends who support each other's growth may engage in conversations about values, goals, and challenges. Helping each other gain clarity about their next steps.

A friend might ask thoughtful questions that encourage self-reflection, such as, "What's something you've always wanted to try but haven't yet?" or "What's a goal you're passionate about that I can support you in?" These questions open the door for meaningful discussions. This helps friends gain insight into their aspirations and find encouragement to pursue them.

A supportive friendship radiates optimism and positivity. Assisting in maintaining hope and resilience even in the face of obstacles. This positivity doesn't mean ignoring challenges; rather, it's about approaching them with a constructive mindset. Permitting each other to see the possibilities and potential within every situation.

One way friends can encourage each other's growth is by focusing on each other's strengths and reminding each other of their abilities. During times of doubt or uncertainty, having a friend who
believes in your strengths can make a significant difference. This focus on strengths also creates a sense of empowerment, where each friend feels confident in their capabilities.

For example, if one friend is facing a difficult career transition, the other might remind them of their resilience, creativity, or adaptability. Highlighting strengths not only boosts morale but also helps friends approach challenges with a renewed sense of confidence.

Practicing Constructive Positivity

Constructive positivity involves looking at challenges with a balanced perspective, acknowledging the difficulty while also focusing on possible solutions or learning opportunities. This type of positivity doesn't dismiss feelings of frustration or disappointment; instead, it encourages friends to see how they might grow or adapt as a result of these experiences.

A friend practicing constructive positivity might say, "I know this setback feels discouraging, but it might be an opportunity to approach things from a different angle. What would help you feel more prepared next time?" This approach fosters resilience and adaptability, helping each friend maintain an optimistic outlook even when faced with setbacks.

Fostering a Friendship That Supports Growth and Goals

Supporting each other's growth and goals within a friendship involves intentional actions and habits. Here's a list of practical steps to create a friendship that encourages both friends to thrive:

1. **Celebrate Each Other's Wins Without Comparison**: When your friend achieves something, celebrate with genuine joy and avoid making comparisons. Treat each achievement as a shared victory and express your excitement in a way that feels meaningful to them.

2. **Show Up Consistently During Challenges**: Be there for your friend during tough times, offering a listening ear and emotional support without judgment. Your presence alone can be a source of strength, showing them that they don't have to navigate their challenges alone.

3. **Encourage Authenticity and Individual Goals**: Support your friend's unique goals, even if they differ from your own. Embrace their individuality, and encourage them to pursue what feels true to them rather than what might be expected or conventional.

4. **Ask Questions That Inspire Self-Reflection**: Engage in conversations that allow your friend to explore their values, dreams, and aspirations. Ask questions that prompt them to reflect on what truly matters to them, helping them gain clarity and motivation.

5. **Remind Each Other of Your Strengths**: During moments of doubt, remind your friend of their strengths and past successes. This affirmation helps boost their confidence and reassures them that they're capable of overcoming obstacles.

6. **Practice Constructive Positivity**: When discussing challenges, focus on potential solutions or learning opportunities rather than solely on the negative aspects. Encourage each other to see the possibilities within setbacks and approach them with resilience.

7. **Respect Boundaries and Offer Support Without Pressure**: Supporting each other's growth also means respecting boundaries. Avoid imposing your own expectations or advice, and instead offer your support in a way that aligns with your friend's comfort level and goals

8. **Check In Regularly on Goals and Progress**: Show interest in your friend's goals by checking in on their progress and offering encouragement. This ongoing support lets them know you're invested in their journey and ready to cheer them on at every step.

9. **Hold Space for Vulnerability and Growth**: Create a safe space where both of you can share your fears, setbacks, and ambitions without fear of judgment. By holding space for each other, you foster an environment where growth can flourish.

10. **Be a Source of Optimism and Hope**: When your friend faces challenges, provide hope and optimism, reminding them that setbacks are temporary and that they have the resilience to overcome them. Your encouragement can be the fuel they need to keep pushing forward. Friendship That Champions Growth and Positivity

Friendships that prioritize growth, optimism, and mutual support create an environment where each person can thrive. Such friendships are rare and precious, offering a partnership that goes beyond shared interests or fun experiences. They're built on a foundation of genuine care, encouragement, and unwavering belief in each other's potential.

When friends actively support each other's growth and goals, they cultivate a bond that is both resilient and inspiring. They become each other's biggest advocates, cheering each other on through triumphs and setbacks, and helping each other evolve into the best versions of themselves. This dynamic not only strengthens the friendship but also enriches each friend's life, creating a relationship that feels like a true partnership in growth and positivity.

Chapter 11

Supporting Dreams

Believing in a friend's aspirations and actively supporting their pursuit can be one of the most profound ways to enrich a friendship. Such dedication deepens trust, inspires growth, and creates a meaningful bond. A bond that is rooted in shared encouragement and hope. When you genuinely stand behind each other's dreams, they become catalysts for each other's success. Thus lifting each other to new heights.

Let's venture into what it means to be the friend who is a steadfast believer in someone else's potential. We'll explore how to provide practical support, unwavering encouragement, and constructive feedback. Ultimately helping and encouraging each other along the path to achieving personal goals. And the journey begins.

Believing and Supporting

Belief in a friend's potential isn't just about saying, "I know you can do it." It's about cultivating a mindset that sees and respects their unique strengths and capabilities. Especially when they might doubt themselves. A belief goes beyond simply sharing uplifting words. It includes acts of respect and dedication to help a friend stay grounded in their journey.

A believing friend has a way of seeing potential that you might overlook or fail to see in yourself. This is especially true during moments of doubt or discouragement. Your supportive friend can become a mirror reflecting the best parts of who you are. You can in turn be the same support for them. In friendships like this, achievements become even more rewarding. These shared victories are celebrated full heartedly.
Supporting a friend's pursuit of their aspirations goes beyond simple words of encouragement. It requires active involvement and thoughtful actions. Actively supporting means looking for ways to help practically, while also

respecting boundaries and never pressuring them to achieve goals on someone else's timeline. Motivation without pressure is a great way to encourage our friends in their endeavors.

Your friend's needs and personality require specific encouragement tailored to them. This lets them know you are in active support of their ambitions. For example, some people thrive on enthusiastic cheering, while others might feel more comfortable with gentle support in the background.

A thoughtful supporter understands when to celebrate big moments and when to remind their friend of past achievements during moments of doubt. This nuanced support lets your friend know they're seen and valued. Especially when progress is slow or obstacles and doubt arise.

Resources and Opportunities

An active supporter keeps an eye out for resources, connections, or opportunities that might help their friend's growth. If you come across a workshop that aligns with your friend's goals, you might share it with them or even attend it together. This type of practical support can make a significant difference, especially when a friend is navigating new challenges.

Sharing resources is a way of saying, "I'm invested in your journey." However, it's essential to offer these suggestions without overwhelming them or overstepping boundaries. The goal here is to present options, not expectations, allowing them to decide what's best for their path. Sometimes, the best way to support a friend's aspirations is by simply listening without judgment or unsolicited advice. Pursuing personal goals can be a vulnerable experience, especially when doubts or fears arise. Listening to their concerns and being present provides a safe space for them to express frustrations and ideas without feeling pressured to produce or perform. This will open new bonding opportunities.

Listening deeply without trying to "fix" things also conveys a powerful message. It says, you are there to support them in whatever capacity they need. Not just as a problem-solver but as a true partner in their journey. You can journey on together.

Constructive Input

Encouragement is essential, but constructive feedback can also be a valuable gift. A friend who genuinely believes in your potential isn't afraid to offer insights that might help you grow. Even if it sometimes requires difficult conversations. Constructive input is about helping each other improve, not bringing each other down.

When giving feedback, it's important to do so with empathy and clarity. Frame it as a perspective that's intended to aid their progress, and reinforce their strengths. An example you might say, "I think this idea is great, and it could be even stronger if you tried [specific suggestion]." Or "I love your passion and creative talent, let me know if I can help you with anything to make sure the task is completed."

Constructive feedback can be one of the strongest ways to show you care. It demonstrates that you're not only invested in their happiness but also in their growth. However, it's vital to ensure that input is always delivered with respect. You must recognize that your friend has the ultimate say in their own journey. It can be helpful to think about what you would want them to say to you in an instance of respectful input for your idea or goal.

Celebrating

Celebrating milestones, both big and small, is an essential part of supporting each other's dreams. Recognizing these special moments reinforces a friend's motivation. It reminds them that their hard work is seen and appreciated.

Major accomplishments are usually built on countless small steps. Acknowledging these small accomplishments can keep a friend's morale high. Sending a simple text noting their progress or treating them to coffee to celebrate a small win. These can be meaningful ways of showing you care.

These small acts of celebration reinforce the idea that every step forward matters. It can be just what they need to make the journey itself feel rewarding, not just the end goal.

When a friend reaches a significant milestone, it's worth creating a memorable celebration to honor their achievement. This can be throwing a small gathering, organizing a dinner, or even giving a thoughtful gift. These special moments of celebration become lasting memories that reinforce the bond between friends.

A powerful message is communicated when you celebrate a friend's big milestones.
Your successes are shared joys, and show that each other's growth is valued. In this way, friends become more than just supporters. You become a part of each other's achievement itself.

Ways to Support Each Other's Aspirations

To actively support each other's goals and aspirations you can implement the listed practical steps below. Insights that can help foster a friendship rooted in mutual encouragement and belief:

1. **Show Genuine Interest in Their Goals**: Ask questions about their aspirations and what drives them. Show that you care by engaging in meaningful conversations about their dreams, helping them clarify their path forward.

2. **Respect Their Individual Journey**: Understand that their timeline and approach might differ from your own. Respect their unique process, offering support without trying to impose your own ideas or expectations.

3. **Celebrate Small Wins Along the Way**: Recognize the importance of progress, no matter how small. Celebrating each step keeps motivation high and reminds your friend that every effort counts.

4. **Provide Constructive Feedback with Empathy**: Offer feedback that is specific, actionable, and rooted in kindness. Frame your suggestions as supportive insights rather than critiques, and always highlight their strengths.

5. **Be Consistent with Your Encouragement**: Show up regularly to encourage them, not just during moments of success but also during times of doubt. Consistent support reinforces your belief in their potential.

6. **Share Resources Thoughtfully**: If you come across articles, events, or tools that align with their goals, share them with an open hand, allowing them to choose what resonates with them.
7. **Create Space for Vulnerability**: Be the kind of friend who welcomes vulnerability, allowing them to express fears, doubts, and frustrations without judgment. A safe space for honesty fosters a stronger connection.

8. **Reaffirm Their Strengths and Capabilities**: Remind them of their past successes and the qualities that make them capable. Your belief in their strengths can be a powerful antidote to self-doubt.

9. **Encourage Reflection and Self-Discovery**: Ask questions that inspire self-reflection, helping them gain clarity about their goals and the steps they want to take. Support their journey toward greater self-awareness.

10. **Celebrate Major Achievements Wholeheartedly**: When they reach a major milestone, celebrate it in a way that feels meaningful to both of you. Make it a memorable occasion that honors their hard work and dedication.

Becoming a True Partner in a Friend's Aspirations

Being a person who believes in your friends aspirations is a profound and generous role to play. It's a commitment to not only supporting their goals but also walking alongside them through every stage of their journey. Walking together through the victories, setbacks, doubts, and achievements. This type of friendship requires consistency, empathy, and a genuine desire to see the other person flourish. You are becoming the best friend someone could aspire to have.

A friendship rooted in mutual support and belief creates a bond that goes beyond typical companionship. It becomes a partnership where both people feel seen, valued, and inspired to become the best versions of themselves. Isn't that something we all truly desire. Another person that is truly in our corner and cheering us on to be the best we can be.The trust, encouragement, and celebration shared in such a friendship cultivate not only personal growth but also a deep and lasting connection that stands the test of time.

Chapter 12

It's A Journey

When we embrace friendship as a lifelong journey, it has the power to continually enrich our lives. Shaping who we are in ways that are profound, fulfilling, and transformative. As life takes us through various stages, our friendships adapt and evolve alongside us. We become pillars of support, sources of joy, and wells of wisdom that we can return to again and again. In conclusion , we'll reflect on the essence of friendship as a journey. A journey marked by change, growth, and the enduring significance of human connection.

Friendship doesn't begin and end in static moments. Rather, it is an ongoing narrative that weaves through the experiences, trials, and triumphs of our lives. The people we consider friends become witnesses to our stories and co-authors of memories that shape the narrative of our lives. If we choose to approach friendship with an understanding of its dynamic nature, we become better equipped to nurture it through all of life's ebbs and flows. In turn recognizing that it is a relationship as alive and growing as we are.

Seasons of Change

As the seasons of our lives change, so too do our friendships. Just as we grow through different phases such as school, careers, relationships, and family. Our friendships reflect these transitions. Some friends walk with us through multiple seasons, adapting and evolving alongside us. Others may come into our lives for a shorter period, yet leave an indelible mark on our hearts. Embracing the seasons of friendship means accepting that, like life itself, relationships grow, shift, and sometimes even fade. However, each one leaves a lasting legacy.

A childhood friend, there for our early formative years, might know us in ways that newer friends may never fully understand,.. College or early adulthood friendships might be filled with exploration and discovery as we shape our identities and start to build our futures. Later, we might find friends in colleagues, fellow parents, or people we connect with over shared passions. These friends see us through different lenses, contributing new perspectives and influences to our lives. Everyone of these friends plays a different and enriching part in our lives.

Each season holds its own beauty and value. Friendships that grow with us through these shifts often become our most cherished ones, as they hold memories from various stages of our lives. The friends who share our early dreams, our big achievements, and our moments of doubt are the ones who understand not only who we are now but also the journey we took to get here. These friends become the mirrors that reflect our growth, showing us how far we've come and how much we have changed over the years.

One of the most profound aspects of friendship is its ability to act as a catalyst for self-discovery and growth. Real true friends not only accept us as we are but also encourage us to become who we aspire to be. They may see us in ways that we sometimes struggle to see ourselves. This allows them to point out strengths we may overlook and gently guide us away from self-doubt. In this journey of friendship, we are granted the space to experiment, to fail, to succeed, and to dream. Knowing along the way we have people who will stand by us through it all.

Friends offer us a unique perspective, as friends have the advantage of being close yet outside observers of our lives. Unlike family, who may have lifelong histories with us, or romantic partners, who share our daily lives, friends have a certain distance that allows them to offer insights we might not otherwise receive. Helping us see our patterns, both positive and negative, and provide a safe space for reflection and growth. The key here is a healthy safe space.

This is the manner in which friendship becomes a mirror for self-discovery. Our friends reveal our blind spots, encouraging us to confront aspects of ourselves we might otherwise ignore. Also celebrating our uniqueness, helping us recognize and value our strengths. When we are uncertain or struggling, it is often our friends who remind us of our worth and capabilities. They can reignite our sense of purpose.
Acceptance is another role friendship plays in self-discovery. True friends embrace us for who we are, flaws and all. This acceptance allows us to be authentic and honest, free from the fear of judgment. In a world where we are often expected to wear masks, friendship offers a sanctuary where we can be our true selves. Combined with encouragement,that acceptance creates fertile ground for personal growth and transformation.

Challenges

No friendship is without its challenges. Disagreements, misunderstandings, and periods of distance are natural in any close relationship. But it is through these challenges that we often find the most significant opportunities for growth, both individually and together. Friends may disappoint us, and we may disappoint them. Expectations might go unmet, and communication may falter. It's the process of navigating these tensions that can strengthen the relationship, building a deeper understanding and appreciation for each other.

The journey of friendship teaches us patience, empathy, and forgiveness. It challenges us to confront our own limitations and biases, as well as to understand and respect those of others. When handled with care, conflicts in friendship become moments of profound learning and connection. They teach us about setting boundaries, expressing our needs, and respecting the perspectives of others. These lessons often extend beyond friendship, enriching our interactions with others in all areas of life.

Forgiveness is perhaps one of the most valuable lessons friendship teaches us. To maintain a long-term friendship, we must learn to let go of grudges, to apologize sincerely, and to forgive fully. This doesn't mean accepting mistreatment; rather, it means understanding that we are all imperfect and that sometimes, we may hurt those we care about. Friends who can forgive and move forward create a resilience within the relationship, knowing it can withstand the occasional storm.

Memories

The memories we create with friends become treasured chapters in the story of our lives. These moments, shared laughter, adventures, and quiet conversations, are the building blocks of our friendships. Weaving a tapestry of shared experiences that only the two of you fully understand. Over time, these memories become touchstones, reminders of the joy, support, and connection that friendship brings.

Many friendships develop their own unique traditions, whether it's a weekly phone call, an annual trip, or a simple tradition like meeting for coffee on the first Sunday of the month. These customs become anchors, offering stability and continuity even as life changes around us. They give us something to look forward to and remind us of the value of consistency in a world that is often unpredictable.

Shared memories and traditions also create a sense of belonging. They remind us that we are part of something bigger than ourselves, connected to another person in a way that is both intimate and lasting. These moments become stories we carry with us, sources of laughter and comfort that we can revisit whenever we need a reminder of the joy and beauty of connection.

Throughout the course of life, we encounter many different kinds of friends. Some friendships are meant to last a lifetime, while others may come and go. Letting go of a friendship, especially one that has played a significant role in our lives, is one of the most difficult yet necessary acts of all. Whether due to growing apart, misunderstandings, or changes in life circumstances, there comes a point when we must acknowledge that a friendship has run its course.

The story of Noah and Riley illustrates this painful reality. They had been inseparable throughout college, sharing everything from study sessions to late-night conversations about their futures. But as they entered their late twenties, their lives began to change in different directions. Noah found himself in a long-term relationship and started a career that required more of his attention, while Riley remained focused on her travels and creative passions.

At first, they tried to keep their bond alive, but the differences in their lifestyles and priorities made it increasingly difficult. They began to drift apart, and the relationship, once full of shared dreams and experiences, felt more like an obligation than a joyful connection. After a particularly strained conversation, they both realized that they had grown into different people, each with new needs and aspirations.

With heavy hearts, they decided to part ways—though not with anger or resentment, but with the mutual understanding that sometimes, the greatest act of friendship is knowing when to let go. It was a painful decision, but one that was necessary for both of them to grow into the people they were meant to be.

And so, Noah and Riley parted ways, but their friendship had not been in vain. In fact, the lessons they learned from each other stayed with them for years to come. They both cherished the memories they had shared and recognized that some friendships, even when they end, serve a greater purpose in shaping who we are.

As we reflect on friendship as a lifelong journey, it's clear that the impact of true friends goes beyond the individual relationship. Friendships have a ripple effect, influencing how we relate to others, how we view the world, and even how we see ourselves. A friend who teaches us kindness, patience, or resilience leaves an imprint on our character. Shaping how we approach other relationships and experiences.

In many ways, our friendships become part of our legacy. The kindness we show, the support we offer, and the memories we create with our friends all contribute to a broader narrative of love and connection. These relationships remind us of our shared humanity, of the importance of empathy and understanding. They help us realize that we are all interconnected, part of a larger tapestry that spans across communities and generations. A connected part of a larger whole.

A friendship that has weathered time and change becomes a testament to the enduring power of human connection. It reminds us that while life is constantly evolving, some bonds remain steadfast. These friendships give us a sense of continuity and belonging, grounding us in a world that is often in flux.

The journey of friendship mirrors the journey of life itself. It is filled with joys and sorrows, triumphs and setbacks, laughter and tears. It requires effort, patience, and a willingness to adapt. Like life, friendship is unpredictable, and its path is rarely linear. But it is precisely this unpredictability that makes friendship so rewarding.
Friendship teaches us that life is meant to be shared, that our experiences are richer when we have someone to share them with. It reminds us that we are not alone, even in our darkest moments. Friends are the ones who walk beside us, who celebrate our successes and comfort us in our losses. They are the ones who remind us of our worth when we forget it ourselves.

In the end, friendship is not defined by perfection but by presence. It is not about never disagreeing or disappointing each other but about being there, consistently and wholeheartedly. It is about showing up, time and again, even when it's difficult. It is about choosing each other, day after day, and valuing the connection enough to work through the challenges.

A Lifelong Journey of Love and Connection

As we reach the end of this reflection on friendship, it's clear that friendship is one of life's greatest gifts. It is a relationship that, when nurtured, has the power to transform our lives in countless ways. It brings joy, meaning, and a sense of belonging, enriching our lives in ways that few other relationships can.

Friendship, in its truest form, is an expression of love. It is a bond that transcends distance, time, and even occasional disagreements. It is a connection that grows and evolves, reflecting the beauty and complexity of life itself. As we journey through life, may we cherish our friendships, nurture them with care, and honor the gift of connection that they represent. For in the end, it is these relationships that leave the deepest imprint on our hearts, reminding us of the joy, resilience, and love that friendship brings to our lives.

As we bring this conversation to a close, it's been a thoughtful journey exploring the nuanced art of friendship and the ways it deeply shapes our lives. Writing about these ideas reflects not just a dedication to creating meaningful content, but also a commitment to honoring the richness of our human connection. This is an endeavor that is as rewarding to contemplate as it is to express.

As we reach the end of this journey, it's essential to acknowledge that friendship is timeless. It is one of those rare gifts that remains with us through the ebbs and flows of life. True friendships are not subject to trends or fleeting moments, they endure. The value of friendship lies not in the number of years we share with someone, but in the depth of connection and mutual respect that we build.

When we reflect on the friendships that have touched our lives, we come to realize that these are the relationships that have had the most lasting impact on us. They are the ones that have shaped us into who we are, provided us with wisdom in moments of confusion, and stood by us when the world felt too heavy to bear alone.

The beauty of friendship is that it can be a constant in a world that often feels in flux. It reminds us that we are not alone. Reminds us that we are worthy of love, and that no matter where life takes us, we will always have a few special people who are willing to walk alongside us, no matter the distance or the time apart.

As you look back on your own friendships, take a moment to appreciate the unique gifts each one has brought into your life. The moments of laughter, the tears shared, the lessons learned, and the growth achieved together. True friendship is not a given, it is something we choose, we nurture, and we treasure. In return, it will continue to shape us, guide us, and remind us of the beauty of being truly seen and truly loved.

Being the ultimate best friend is not about perfection, it's about effort, intention, and love. It's about showing up, day after day, with empathy, kindness, honesty, and respect. It's about creating a safe space where both you and your friend can grow, make mistakes, and become better versions of yourselves. Through consistency, grace, boundaries, and encouragement, you build a friendship that endures, one that is rich with depth and meaning.

This book is written for those navigating normally healthy, non-toxic relationships—where love, respect, and growth are present, even if imperfect. But it also serves as a guide to help you recognize when something shifts. If your voice is silenced, your worth constantly questioned, or your peace repeatedly disturbed, it's time to look deeper. Knowing when to walk away isn't weakness—it's wisdom. A healthy relationship challenges you, but it never harms you.

As you embark on this journey of becoming the ultimate best friend, remember that it's not a destination, but a continuous process. A process of learning, of evolving, and of loving with everything you have. This guidebook is not just a tool for improving your friendships, it is a reminder that the art of being a great friend is one of life's most beautiful and rewarding experiences.

In these explorations, each concept and detail is designed to help you find value, resonance, and perhaps a renewed perspective on your own relationships. With these reflections, I hope this book on friendship will offer a lasting resource, encouraging you to deepen your own friendships and find joy in the lifelong journey of connection.

Thank you for engaging so deeply in the process and for exploring the beauty of friendship with me. May these reflections inspire deeper connections and remind you of the incredible value of true companionship. I truly hope it leads you to a life full of true meaningful relationships. For an added resource please use the companion journal.

A friend loves at all times   Proverbs 17
Oil and perfume make the heart glad, and the sweetness of a friend comes from their earnest counsel. Proverbs 27:9
Therefore encourage one another and build each other up, just as you are doing. 1 Thessalonians 5:11
Bear with each other and forgive one another Colossians 3:13
Two are better than one….if they fall down one can help the other up Ecclesiastes 4

Also available for purchase is the companion journal to complement this book. Enjoy!

Resources

The role of friendships in well-being
Fehr, B., & Harasmychuk, C. In Maddux, J. E. (Ed.), *Subjective Well-Being and Life Satisfaction, Routledge*, 2017

Beyond the isolated brain: The promise and challenge of interacting minds
Wheatley, T., et al., *Neuron*, 2019

Adult friendship and wellbeing: A systematic review with practical implications
Pezirkianidis, C., et al., *Frontiers in Psychology*, 2023

What prevents people from making friends: A taxonomy of reasons
Apostolou, M., & Keramari, D., *Personality and Individual Differences*, 2020

The science of why friendships keep us healthy American culture prioritizes romance, but psychological science is exploring the human need for platonic relationships and the specific ways in which they bolster well-being
By Zara AbramsDate created: June 1, 2023

UVA Today: Human Brains Are Hardwired for Empathy, Friendship, Study Shows By Fariss Samarrai, farisss@virginia.edu   August 21, 2013

Psychologists' research offers insight into why it's so important to practice the "right" kind of empathy, and how to grow these skills American

Psychological Association By <u>Ashley Abramson</u>Date created: November 1, 2021

Harvard Health Blog   The heart and science of kindness April 18, 2019
By <u>Melissa Brodrick, MEd</u>, Contributor

Friendships enrich your life and improve your health

Assiste ai outline

Discover the connection between health and friendship, and how to promote and maintain healthy friendships. <u>By Mayo Clinic Staff</u>

Also available for purchase is the companion journal to complement this book. Enjoy!

One who has unreliable friends soon comes to ruin,
*   but there is a friend who sticks closer than a brother. Proverbs 18*
Perfume and incense bring joy to the heart,
*   and the pleasantness of a friend*
*   springs from their heartfelt advice.*
As iron sharpens iron,
*   so one person sharpens another. Proverbs 27*
* Do to others as you would have them do to you. Luke 6*
Listen to advice and accept discipline,
*   and at the end you will be counted among the wise.*
Many are the plans in a person's heart,
*   but it is the Lord's purpose that prevails. Proverbs 19*
Walk with the wise and become wise,
*   for a companion of fools suffers harm. Proverbs 13*
My intercessor is my friend
*   as my eyes pour out tears to God;*
on behalf of a man he pleads with God
*   as one pleads for a friend. Job 16*